PUBLISHED FOR THE MALONE SOCIETY BY
OXFORD UNIVERSITY PRESS

WALTON STREET, OXFORD OX2 6DP

Oxford   New York   Toronto
Delhi   Bombay   Calcutta   Karachi
Petaling Jaya   Singapore   Hong Kong   Tokyo
Nairobi   Dar es Salaam   Cape Town
Melbourne   Auckland

and associated companies in
Berlin   Ibadan

ISBN 0 19 7290299

Printed by BAS Printers Limited, Over Wallop, Hampshire

TWO MORAL INTERLUDES

THE MALONE SOCIETY
REPRINTS
1991

THESE editions of *Witty and Witless* by John Heywood, and *Like Will to Like* by Ulpian Fulwell, were prepared by Peter Happé. H. R. Woudhuysen and the General Editor assisted with their preparation, and checked the editions.

The Society is grateful to the British Library for permission to edit the text and reproduce pages from its manuscript, Harley 367 (for *Witty and Witless*). It is grateful to the Bodleian Library, Oxford for permission to reproduce its copy of the 1568 quarto edition of *Like Will to Like* (Malone 231(3)); and to the Folger Shakespeare Library, Washington DC for permission to reproduce pages from its copy of the undated second quarto.

January 1991   JOHN PITCHER

CONTENTS

WITTY AND WITLESS
BY
JOHN HEYWOOD

INTRODUCTION

The Manuscript: Provenance and Physical Description

THE interlude known as *Witty and Witless* is transcribed on Fols. 110–19 of the British Library manuscript, Harley 367. This is a collection of separate papers and letters. The *Witty and Witless* manuscript, which is untitled, is situated between manuscripts of Skelton's *Ageinst Lusty Garnyshe* and the poem *Flowden Feilde*. Harley 367, or part of it, was first assembled by John Stowe, the antiquarian (1525–1605). It passed through the hands of Ralph Starkey of Darley Hall, Oulton (d. 1628), and from there to the library of Sir Simonds D'Ewes (1602–50). Robert Harley acquired the collection from a grandson of Sir Simonds in 1705.[1] It is not clear when Harley 367 was bound, nor at what point the manuscript of *Witty and Witless* was incorporated into the collection, although there is evidence that Fols. 101–87 were already to be found together in the D'Ewes library.[2]

The first known reference to the interlude appears in the manuscript catalogue compiled for Robert Harley by Humphrey Wanley between 1708 and 1726. In this, Item 42 of Harley 367 is described as:

John Heywode Poetical Dialogue concerning Witty (i.e. Wise,) & Witless: <u>made, as it seems, to be recited before K.Henry VIII. fol.110</u>.[3]

This was repeated in the printed catalogues of the Harleian collection in 1759 and 1808, where the play was given the number 41. The modern title *Witty and Witless* is derived from Wanley's description.

The ten leaves of the manuscript, now mounted as bifolia, measure approximately 307 × 205 mm. They are numbered 110–119 in pencil on each recto. Fol. 110a is soiled and darkened, and Fol. 119 shows signs of damp. The leaves have been folded vertically, and it is possible that the blank page at the end, Fol. 119b, served at some stage as an outside cover. The paper appears to date from the middle of the sixteenth century. The watermark consists of a hand with fingers together and the thumb outstretched, and a five-pointed star or flower at the extension of the longest finger. In the palm and wrist of the hand is the number '3' and the initials 'HA'. This corresponds most closely to Briquet, Numbers 11377–82, which suggests an origin for the paper in the north-west

---

[1] See C. E. Wright, *Fontes Harleiani* (London, 1972), p. 378.

[2] See A. G. Watson, *The Library of Sir Simonds D'Ewes* (London, 1966), p. 157.

[3] British Library Additional MS. 45702, Fol. 50a. There is a reference to a 'Playe of wytles' in the Stationers' Register for 1560/1: see W. W. Greg, *A Bibliography of the English Printed Drama to the Restoration*, 4 vols. (London, 1939–59), i. 2.

of France. Briquet's examples date between 1547 and 1559.[4] It has been suggested that this watermark occurs (among others) in the British Library manuscript, Royal 7. B. iv, Cranmer's draft of the Prayer Book, 1543–7,[5] but there are slight variations in the design of the hand, and the chainlines in the papers are different (Harley 367 = 20 mm; Royal 7. B. iv. = 28 mm.). In Harley 367, the watermark appears on Fols. 111, 114, 116, 117, 119, which may indicate that the manuscript was first made up as a single gathering of ten leaves in twos. In Fols. 111 and 114 the hand points up the page rather than down.

THE HAND

The text of the interlude is subscribed 'Iohn heywod', but it has been shown that this is not an autograph: it is quite unlike the example of Heywood's signature on a lease dated 20 February 1538/9.[6] *Witty and Witless* is written in a Tudor secretary hand, which is distinguished by such letters as the tailed 'h', the long 's', the 'c' in two strokes, and the reversed 'e'. There are three forms for the letter 's': the differences between them can be seen in the words 'sott' (and 'saythe'), 'as', and 'wyttes' in l. 22 (illustrated in Plate 1). The letter 'y' is almost always dotted, which may well be a medieval feature—it is one which the scribe shares with the poet Hoccleve, for example, who was a professional scribe.[7] This feature helps to distinguish 'y' from the tailed 'n' which has no dot. In a number of cases the scribe has carefully added a tail to 'n' (with 'evyn' in l. 112, for example). Perhaps the most difficult aspect of the handwriting is the indeterminate nature of final 'e'. In the clearest examples there is a curl which adequately and undoubtedly represents this letter, but there is a problem when the curl is flattened to a dash: compare 'welthe' with 'wewe' in l. 13, and 'the' in ll. 668 and 669 (illustrated in Plates 1 and 2). A comparable difficulty occurs with 'c' in words such as 'schowe', where the letter is frequently not much more than a minute vertical stroke attached to the horizontal beginning of the 'h' (see 'schowe' in l. 14 and 'schowthe' in l. 671). By contrast with these, the character for 're' was formed with great consistency

[4] C. M. Briquet, *Les Filigranes*, ed. Allan Stevenson, 4 vols. (Amsterdam, 1968). In 'Sources of Early English Paper-Supply', *The Library*, 4th series, x (1930), 427–54, Edward Heawood identifies this type of watermark in manuscripts from 1531 to 1574, and in printed books from 1530 (Rastell's *Purgatory*) to as late as 1590. He agrees that the paper is from north-west France (see pp. 437–8, and his fig. 137).

[5] Noted by J. A. Herbert in *Witty and Witless*, ed. J. S. Farmer, Tudor Facsimile Texts (London, 1909), p. v.

[6] See A. W. Reed, *Early Tudor Drama* (London, 1926), pp. 123–4.

[7] See P. J. Croft, *Autograph Poetry in the English Language*, 2 vols. (London, 1973), i. 3–4 (and also the piece by William Herbert, d. 1333?).

throughout the text, and it can normally be distinguished quite easily from the letter 'r': examples are 'resurrectyon' in l. 673, and 'trewer' in l. 14, which have both letter shapes. There are a number of instances where the scribe has emended the character for 're' to make it clear that a letter 'e' is present (with 'entre' and 'prefe', ll. 523 and 554 respectively).

The most intriguing feature of this hand is its formation of the majuscule 'I'. This is made in two ways. In one form, the letter begins (on the line, or slightly above or below it) as a curved stroke turning upwards from the left to the apex, followed by a long downward stroke which curves to the left again, loops back, and passes across itself on the line. The head of the letter is normally open, although there are instances where the initial and final positions of the pen are very close. This is the form (A) used in 'Iames' and 'Iohn', in ll. 5 and 9, and the first 'I' in l. 6 (see Plate 1). With the other form (B), used for 'Iohn' in l. 1, and the second 'I' in l. 6, the scribe carries the first curve further to the right, and then draws it back quite sharply into an almost vertical downward stroke: at the base of the letter, this stroke turns up and to the left, and ends in a plump loop.

What is interesting about these two forms, A and B, is the pattern of their use. In the text there are 102 instances of the names 'Iohn', 'Iames', and 'Ierome', and their abbreviated forms (one hundred in the speech prefixes, two in the speeches). The scribe uses the B form of 'I' in only five cases, one of which is in l. 1, and another a deletion (in l. 270). It is tempting to think that there may be something more to this than merely the scribe's preference for one writing shape over another. Might it be that he was attempting to distinguish, albeit not quite consistently, between the letters 'I' and 'J', as we now do in modern spelling? It is possible that he intended the A form of 'I' to be taken for a 'J'. The accepted scholarly view of the distinction between 'I' and 'J' in hands of this period is summarized by Dawson and Kennedy-Skipton. They write that, under the influence of Latin,

these two letters (as we consider them to be) were always, at least down to the seventeenth century, regarded as two forms of the same letter. As a consonant (*jump*) the letter was pronounced as we pronounce *j*, but in the sixteenth century most writers and most printers always used *i* instead of *j*, either vowel or consonant, both initially and medially. Of the capital letter only one written form existed, and few printers' fonts seem even to have contained a *J*. . . . In transcribing *J* either *I* or *J* may be used, but not both; *I* is generally preferred.[8]

Against this, one might venture that the Tudor hand in *Witty and Witless* was one in transition from old to new practice. There is indeed evidence that at

[8] Giles E. Dawson and Laetitia Kennedy-Skipton, *Elizabethan Handwriting 1500–1650* (London, 1968), p. 14.

around the same time (in *c.*1541) Udall was using two similar letter forms for 'I'.[9]

It is the pattern of use for words other than Christian names which shows the scribe's practice to be less modern. Let us suppose, for a moment, that the A letter shape 'I' = 'J', and the B shape 'I' = 'I'. At first the frequency of agreement with modern spellings seems impressive. Take Fol.117b, for example, where there are sixteen of these majuscules (other than those used for names) in forty-five lines (ll. 678–722), in this sequence: 'J', 'I', 'In', 'In', 'Iustyce', 'I', 'J', 'J', 'Joy', 'I', 'I', 'I', 'Joyes', 'Joyes', 'J', 'Joy'. There is inconsistency, of course, but at least two-thirds of these follow the modern convention. The same proportion of modern to unmodern usage occurs throughout the text, in around 280 cases. Equally notable is the preference for the A form in initial consonants (all but two of thirty-nine instances). What is less impressive is the scribe's failure to distinguish these letters when he is copying the same or a similar word. Maintaining the distinction of 'I' and 'J', as above, we find 'Joyne' with 'Ioyne' (ll. 100 and 124) 'Imagynacyon' with 'Jmagynacyon', and later 'Jmagynashyon' (ll. 305, 318, and 574), and 'Justyce' with 'Iustyce' (ll. 651 and 695). Faced with these and other examples, the best one can say for the scribe's modernity over 'I' and 'J' is that he may have wished to differentiate the letters in certain cases, most especially with personal names, but that generally he has no clear and uniform practice. It would be unwise not to follow the view of Dawson and Kennedy-Skipton in editing this aspect of the text, although a record of the occurrences of the B variant does seem appropriate (see p. 15).

The scribe drew lines and flourishes over many words in the text. Particularly frequent are the ones above 'hym', and above words which include 'yn' and 'en'. Most of these lines are otiose,[10] and significant only where they are abbreviations or brevigraphs for omitted letters. The conventional abbreviations present few difficulties: 'yᵉ' (for 'the'), 'ẏ' ('that'), 'ẇ' ('with'), 'wᶜʰᵉ' ('which'), 'yoʳ' ('your'), 'ꝓ' ('pro'), 'ꝑa' ('pra'), 'ẹ' (final 'es'). One brevigraph, for 'ra', appears to be an 'a' elongated into a dash at its head (with 'gcys' for 'grace's', l. 50; 'py' for 'pray', ll. 516 and 523; 'gce' for 'grace', ll. 736 and 741). Sometimes this mark is superfluous, with 'grace' in ll. 786 and 797, and above 'sum' in ll. 644 and 668 (see below, Editorial Conventions).

The cursive nature of the hand causes words to run into each other from time to time. On occasions the scribe has taken care to divide these joins by drawing an oblique line through them ('Ye/schow', and 'grawnt/and' in ll. 10 and 676,

---

[9] See W. W. Greg, *et al.*, *English Literary Autographs*, 3 parts (Oxford, 1925–32), i. no. xxxii.
[10] Cf. A. G. Petti, *English Literary Hands from Chaucer to Dryden* (London, 1977), no. 20, dated 1545.

for example: see Plates 1 and 2 respectively). He also uses an oblique line or virgule as the equivalent of a comma or a full stop (for example, 'one yoke / for thynke', l. 616). Speeches are separated by lines drawn freehand across the page. These run into the speech prefixes, which are set slightly above and to the right of the body of the speeches. On Fols. 116a, 117b, and 118b, where a speech begins at the top of the page, the speaker's name is given twice: in the right margin at the foot of the previous page, and then again centred above the speech itself (ll. 536–7, 677–8, and 763–4). Since the play opens in this way, on Fol. 110a, with a speech prefix in the centre of the page (see Plate 1), it is possible that some text has been lost at its beginning. The argument of the play does seem complete, however, even though the action begins with a conversation already in progress. There are no catchwords in the manuscript.

In general the text was prepared with care. There are generous margins to the left and right of the speeches, and at the foot of the page. The text was copied out at around forty to forty-five lines per page, and the scribe's corrections suggest that he paid close attention to what he was copying. He corrected errors caused by eyeskip (see ll. 260 and 316), and he appears to have been particularly concerned with the formation of certain letters (as with ^{1}e in 'plesewre' in l. 552). Several of his alterations reveal a concern with spelling. He changed 'way' to 'wey' (l. 347); 'w' to 'wh' and 'wh' to 'w' (ll. 196 and 481); 'mayny' to 'many' (l. 322); 'best' to 'beast' (l. 543); 'u' to 'ew' (l. 188); 'dylayte' to 'dylate' (l. 284); and 'reson' to 'reason' (l. 206). Several times he clarified 'ea' in 'reason' and doubled the letters 'o', 't', 'r', and 'l'. Inconsistencies remain, however, most notably with the words 'thynke' and 'thyng'. He writes 'thyngke' in ll. 90 and 550, corrects 'thyngke' to 'thynke' in l. 385, and 'thyngks' to 'things' in l. 551, but leaves 'Thyng' (for 'Think') uncorrected in l. 161. He is also inconsistent with words which in modern English end in 'ble': see honorabull' (l. 115), 'vnmesewrabull' (l. 240), 'tabyll' (l. 116), 'sensybyll' (l. 552, twice), 'resonabyll' (l. 574), and 'resonable' (l. 526). Most of the corrections in the manuscript seem to have been made while the text was being copied, but a few of them may have been added subsequently (in l. 316, for example).

THE PLAY

It is reasonable to accept that John Heywood wrote the play, even though there is no contemporary external evidence to support the attribution. The style and content of *Witty and Witless* are consistent with what we find in other plays by Heywood, especially in the patterning of words (see, for example, the use of 'sey', 'seyde', and 'seynge' in ll. 222–6), and in the balancing of viewpoints between characters (which recalls the arrangement in his *The Play of Love* and

13

The Play of the Weather).[11] The play is unquestionably Catholic in outlook (see ll. 384–99), and its author shows signs of having been influenced by French and humanist thought, rather than the English morality tradition. Its subject is one which would have appealed to the cultural milieu of Erasmus and More, with which Heywood is known to have been associated. The only evidence for its date are the references to Will Somer (l. 779 etc.) who arrived at court in 1525. From the direction at ll. 798–9 one can deduce that *Witty and Witless* was intended for performance before the King. This is usually taken to be Henry VIII. In 1528 Heywood was discharged from the court with a pension, but he continued to make appearances in connection with court entertainments until much later. The play may have contributed to Heywood's support for his kinsman More in religious and political matters in the late 1520s and early 1530s. There were, however, differences between them. More's writing at this time was polemical and abrasive; by contrast, Heywood's was tolerant, good humoured and diplomatic, consonant with his life as a courtier. No specific source for the play has yet been discovered, although there are several analogues.[12] Its argument, and its place in Heywood's life and work, have received some attention from scholars in recent years.[13] The most recent text of *Witty and Witless* was published over fifty years ago.[14]

EDITORIAL CONVENTIONS

The text has been edited using the following conventions. Each line of text, including the speech prefixes in the right-hand margin, is numbered separately. Numbering is consecutive from the beginning to the end of the play. Square brackets enclose deletions, except for those around the folio numbers, and the description of the final page ([FOL. 119b] etc., and [BLANK]). Angle brackets enclose material which other causes (paper damage, blotting, etc.) have removed or made impossible to decipher; dots indicate illegible characters (thus ⟨.⟩). The virgule, and the oblique line drawn between words, are printed in as exact

[11] See Rupert de la Bère, *John Heywood, Entertainer* (London, 1937), pp. 56–68.

[12] A useful collection of analogues is gathered together by K. W. Cameron in *The Background of Heywood's Witty and Witless* (Raleigh, NC, 1941).

[13] In particular from Joel B. Altman, *The Tudor Play of Mind* (Berkeley and Los Angeles, 1978), pp. 108–12.

[14] The text was first published, in a shortened version for the Percy Society (vol. 20), as *A Dialogue on Wit and Folly by John Heywood*, ed. F. W. Fairholt (London, 1846). J. S. Farmer included it in his collection of modernized texts, *The Dramatic Writings of John Heywood* (London, 1905), pp. 191–217. In 1909 Farmer also produced the Tudor Facsimile Text referred to in n. 5. The play was last edited in 1937, in an old-spelling text, by de la Bère, pp. 115–43 (reference in n. 11). A further old-spelling edition, in *The Plays of John Heywood*, edited by Richard Axton and Peter Happé, and to be published by Boydell and Brewer, is forthcoming. The place of *Witty and Witless* in Heywood's life and work is considered there in more detail.

positions as type will permit. Where the line was used to separate words which had been mistakenly joined, this is rendered here without spacing; the virgule is signalled by spacing on either side of it (for examples of both see l. 56). Throughout the text there are marks which seem to resemble modern punctuation (see, for example, ll. 7 and 22 in Plate 1). These are probably no more than points made when the scribe allowed his pen to rest on the paper in the course of transcription: as such they have been omitted. Lines and flourishes written above words are ignored unless it is certain or very likely that they are signs for omitted or doubled letters (so 'nōbyr' in l. 90, which stands for 'nombyr'). The brevigraph used for 'ra' is marked in all cases, and is represented by an apostrophe printed in 18pt bold-face type.

As with any transcription, several letter shapes require editorial judgements, especially in distinguishing majuscule from minuscule forms (in this hand, this is particularly true for 'a', 'y', and 'w'). The letter 'y', which is almost always dotted, is printed in this edition without a dot. Square 's' represents all three minuscule forms of this letter. The short bar linking 'll' has been ignored (its function was perhaps to distinguish it from 'tt'). The A and B forms of 'I', discussed above pp. 11–12, are both printed here as 'I'. Below there is a list which records every instance of the B form (to show what may be learnt from this scribe's practice, however erratic, about the development of the difference between 'I' and 'J'). The crosses marked in pencil in the margins of the manuscript may be the work of a modern editor, since they are near to lines which might require annotation or emendation (one is beside a proverb, two by Walsingham, and four alongside Somer). The textual notes record where the crosses appear. The portions of text in Plates 1 and 2 are reproduced full-size, with the margins omitted.

Words in the manuscript which have the B form of letter 'I':

1 Iohn	224 I	446 I	694 In
6 ²I	227 I	455 I	695 Iustyce
16 In	250 In	459 I	696 I
26 In	270 [Ih] Iohn	461 Iohn	699 I
28 In	272 I	464 I	700 I
82 I	275 In	468 Ierome	716 I
96 I	287 Insydently	485 In	728 In
98 Inowgh	305 Imagynacyon	499 I	729 In
124 Ioyne	315 Inwarde	503 I	750 I
136 I	329 I	509 I	772 In
155 In	346 I	520 I	777 I
208 I	373 I	551 In	780 In
215 I	388 Infants	639 In	781 I
220 In	389 In	689 I	
222 [I] I	436 I	693 In	

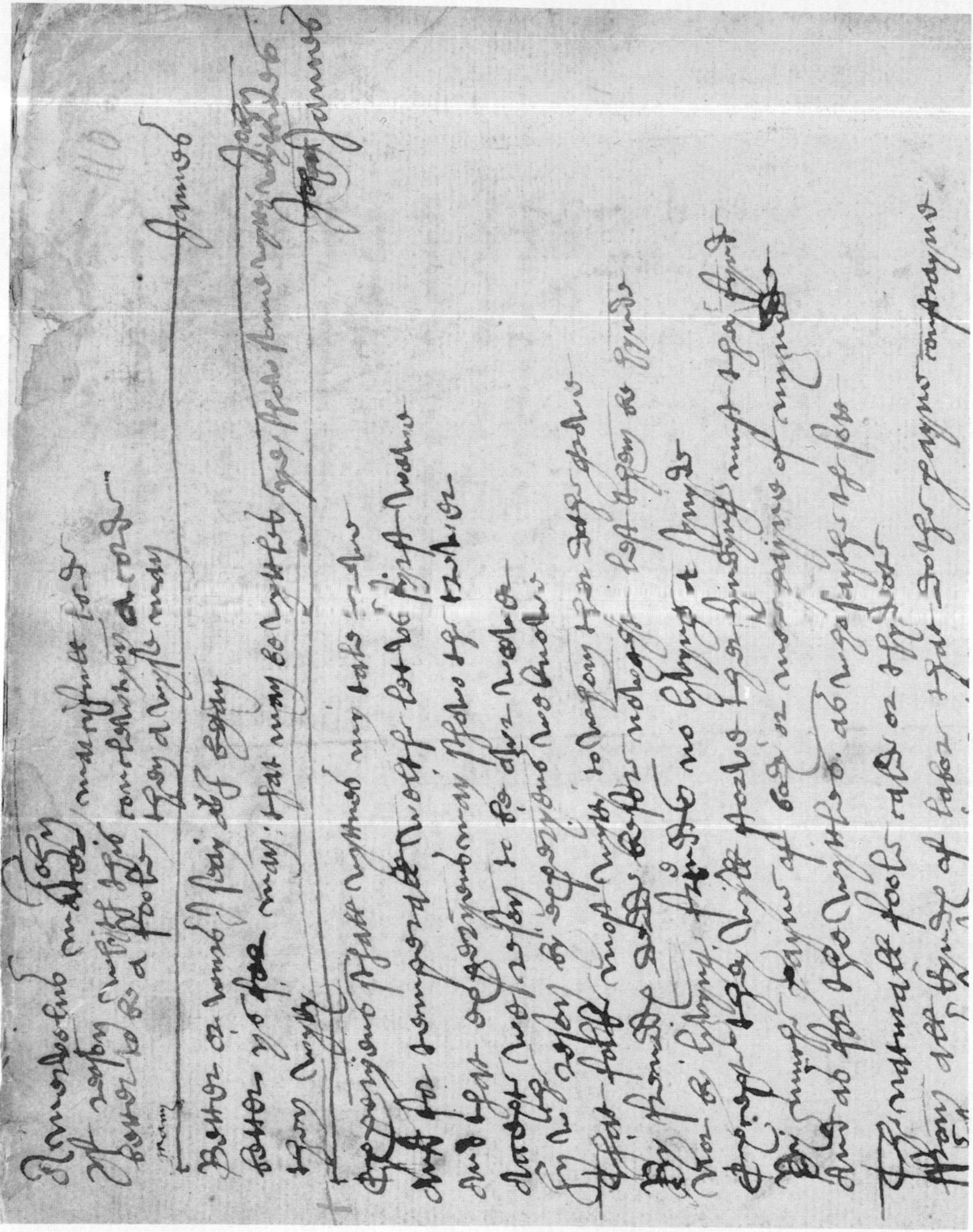

PLATE 1: BRITISH LIBRARY MANUSCRIPT, HARLEY 367, PORTION OF FOL. 110a:
WITTY AND WITLESS, LINES 1 TO 24

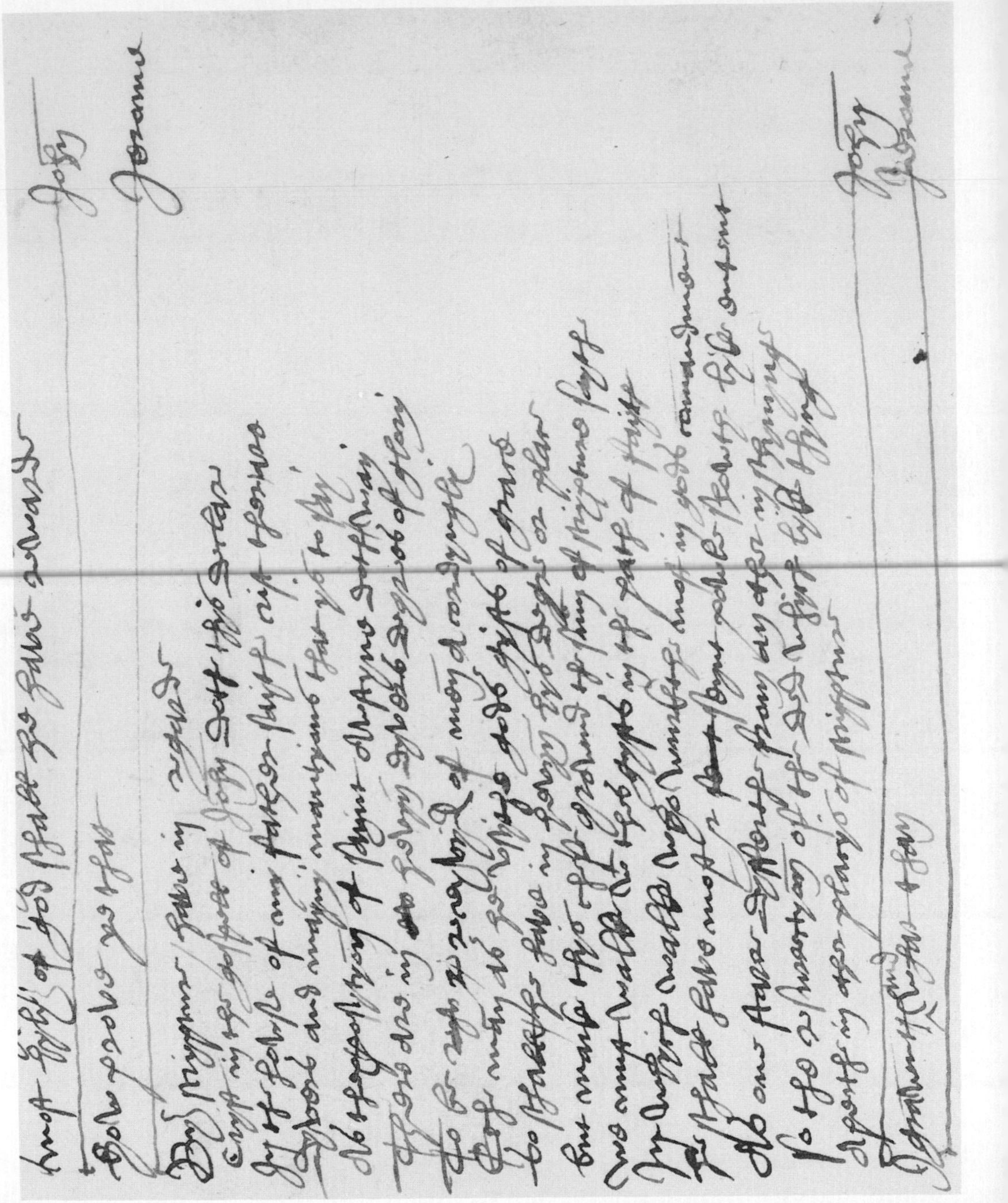

PLATE 2: PORTION OF FOL. 117a: *WITTY AND WITLESS*, LINES 655 TO 677

Iohn
A mervelus mater / marcyfull lorde
Yf reason whyth this conclewtyon a corde
better to be a foole / then a wyse man

———————————————————————————Iames

Better or wurs I seay as I began
better ys for man that man be wyttles
then wytty

———————————————————————————Iohn

Ye / schow some wytty wyttines 10

———————————————————————————[Iohn] Iames

Experyens schall wyttnes my tale trewe
And for temperall welthe let vs fyrst wewe
And that experyens may schowe the trewer
Accepte we reson to be owr wewer
In w^che reson by experyens we knowe
That folke most wytty to whom ther dothe growe
By frendde dedde before nowght left them be hynde
Nor by lyvyng frendds no lyvynge a synyde
Excepte they wyll storve ther fyndyng must they fynde 20
By muche payne of body or more payne of myndde
And as for the wyttles as who saythe the sott
The naturall foole calde or thydeote
ffrom all kynde of labore that dothe payne constrayne
As farre as suffycyency nedythe obtayne
In sewrty of lyvyng the sot dothe remayne

———————————————————————————[Iames] Iohn

In sewrty of lyvyng but not ẘ owt payne

3 *a*] heavily inked   3–4 *m* in left margin, in a later, smaller hand, between these lines
4 *better*] *many* in a later, smaller hand beneath this word   6 *as*] *s* ill formed   *began*] *e*
cramped   9–10 these lines added in right margin in paler ink (the ink pales to this strength
at the foot of Fol. 110b, ll. 79–81); a cross is drawn in ink by the scribe in the left margin beside
l. 10 (see Plate 1)   15 *wewer*] ¹*e* altered, possibly from *a* to *o*   19 *frendds*] *e* interlined
above blot, with caret: perhaps an alteration of the *re* character   21 *myndde*] *dd* altered and
blotted   27 *Iohn*] interlined above deletion, with caret

ffor admyte all sotts in case as be mayny
That leve ẘ owt labor / yet where ys any   30
But for that one plesewr / he hathe more payne
Then the wyty wurker in all dothe sustayne
What wretche so ferythe payne havȳn eny wytt
lyke the wyttles wretche / none yf ye marke hyt
who cumth by the sott who cumth he by
That vexyth hym not somewey vsewally
Some beate hym some bob hym
Some Ioll hym some Iob hym
Some tugg hym by the heres
Some lugg hym by the [ears] eares   40
Some spet at hym some spurne hym
Some tosse hym some turne hym
Some snape hym some snatche hym
~~Some crampe hym some cratche hym~~
Some Cuff some clowt hym
Some lashe hym some lowte hym   [FOL. 110b]
Some whysk hym some whype hym
W[h]ythe
Wythe scharpe naylys some nype hym
Not evyn mayster somer the kyngs ǵcys foole   50
But tastythe some/tyme some nyps of new schoole
And by syd thys kynde of frettyng & fewmyng
Another kynd of turment in consewmyng
The wytty to the wyttles oft Invent
After Inventyon of yerfull entent
The foole / by flatery to turment/ys browght

29 *admyte*] *t* blotted, *e* perhaps added   30 *leve* *ẘ*] ²*e* and *w* perhaps joined
32 *wyty*] ²*y* written over a second *t*   33 *What*] *a* cramped, and a cross pencilled in left margin
48 *W[h]ythe*] abandoned with ¹*h* deleted and *e* incomplete   50 cross pencilled in left margin
51 *schoole*] *h* mended, ¹*o* has a loop as though for *l*, but abandoned   53 cross pencilled
in left margin   *turment*] *n* altered from *m*   55 *yerfull*] possibly *yerefull*   56 *foole*] ¹*o*
blotted

so farre over Ioyd and his brayne/so wyde wrowght
That by Ioy of a Iewell skant wurthe a myght
The sott ofte slepythe no wynke in a whole nyght
And for ensampyll wythe a walsyngam rynge   60
Thys dystemperans to the sot ye may bryng
And make hym Ioy theryn as hyt ware a thyng
Of pryce to peyse the rawnsome of a kynge
In Ioying wherof yf ony man got way
To g[⟨o⟩]et yt from hym as evry chylde may
Then man & chylde sethe the sot in suche case
That nowght but paynfull sorow takythe ony place
By thys small prosses a small wytt may ges
That wyde were the wytty to wyshe them wyttles

————————————————————————————————————Iames   70

Theffecte of this yowr matter as ye spake yt
Standyth muche yn two poynts as I take yt
Of whych tweyne the tone ys that the sot hathe
by Iollynge & Iobbynge and other/lyke skathe
extreme payne wythe the extremyte of yere
Thother ys aft^e frettyng fewryus fyer
That thefoole ẘ eche frewtles tryflyng toy
ys so dystempryd ẘ dystemperat Ioy
That as muche payne brynght his plesaunt passhyon
as dothe the pynchynge of hys most paynfull fashyon   80
Thes two poynts consyderyd the sot as ye saye
hathe some payne somtyme but most tymes I say nay   [FOL. 111a]

————————————————————————————————————Iohn

Then from no payne to some payne the wyttles are browght

————————————————————————————————————Iames

Ye but wytty and wyttles wytyly wrowght

60 cross pencilled in left margin   65 g[⟨o⟩]et] e interlined above blotted letter, perhaps e written over o   71 yt] t written over another letter   72 two] w altered from o
78 dystempryd] e blotted   79 passhyon] ²s probably altered from h   84 Then] tail of h altered   86 Ye] Y perhaps y   wytyly] ²y written over a second t

21

By some payne to suche payne that wytty fele most
Then wytty and wyttles eche parte his parte bost
Take / of wytty the degrees and nombyr all
and of y̏ nombyr I thyngke yᵉ nōbyr small   90
But that eche one of them ys of nede asynde
To labor sore yn body or ells yn mynde
And few to all that fortewne so dothe favor
But yn body & mynde bothe they do labor
And of body thes labors the most paynefullest
ys the labor of mynde I have harde gest
And lest bothe paynes or most of twayne be to towgh[t]
ffor yow to matche w̏ / and the lest payne Inowgh
To the fyrst [payne &] / most payne of yᵉ wyttles nody
Ioyne we the wyttyse least payne[⟨.⟩] / payne of body   100
who sethe what payne labor bodyly bryngth
Schall ~~eaaely~~ ~~te~~ ~~thurby~~ how the body wryngth
husbond mens plowyng or earyng and sowyng
hedgyng and dychyng w̏ repyng and mowyng
In car[⟨.⟩]tyng such lyftyng such burdenns bareyng
That payne of the body bryngthe [thyese] thyese/to stareyng
And muche of thys done yn tyme of suche hete
That yn colde cave covryd the carcas must swete
Some other vse crafts In wᶜʰᵉ [w] / wurcke ys so small
That yn somer plesaunttly they lyve all   110
Who / in wynter when husbondmen warme w̏ warke
In that they may [not] not sturr[⟨.⟩] for colde ar evyn starke
Some yn wynter fryse some yn somer fry

87 *most*] *st* perhaps altered   89 *nombyr*] *y* altered from *e*   90 *nōbyr*] line above *o* inked
more definitely than in most other instances   95 *body*] error for *bothe* (eyeskip from l. 94)
97   *towgh[t]*] deletion not certain, but required by rhyme   99 *[payne &]*] crossed through
and each letter deleted with a vertical stroke   100 *payne[⟨.⟩]*] deleted letter perhaps a long *s*
101 *bodyly*] ¹*y* blotted   102 *Schall*] *c* blotted   104 *dychyng*] ¹*y* altered from *e*
105 *car[⟨.⟩]tyng*] *t* interlined above caret; deleted letter perhaps *r*   106 *stareyng*] *e* interlined above caret   108 *covryd*] *d* blotted   109 *wurcke*] *c* interlined above caret
110 *plesaunttly*] ¹*t* interlined   112 *evyn*] *v* altered, tail added to *n*

And the wyttles dothe nother / for comenly
Other whythe wurshypfull or honorabull
he temprately standth in howse at the tabyll
And of all his labors reckyn the hole rabyll
Bygger burden barthe he nonethen his babyll
So that from thes paynes or the lyke recytyd
The wyttles hathe warrant to be a quyghtyd   120
And sewr the sotts pleasewre in this last aquyghtall   [FOL. 111b]
Cownterwaylth his payne in yowr fyrst recyghtall
Feor vnto the sotts nyppyng and beatyng
Ioyne the wytty laborers nypps and freatyng
And whether ye cownt by [⟨.⟩]yere monthe or weke
ye schall fynde thease of yᵉ wytty to seeke
As far as of the wyttles and of bothe sorts
This ys the dyfferens that to/me ymports
Sotts are coylde of other / the wytty coylthe hym self
What choyse thus A leagyd   130
───Iohn

Small / ah horson elfe
Some what he towchythe me now yn very deed
how [beyt] beyt to thys am not I yet full agreed
The wytty who beate them selves by bysynes
May ofte yn beatyngs favowr them selves I ges
Such oporte[e]wnyte by wytte ys ofte espyde
[In takynge tyme or placs as best may stand]
That labor by wytt ys ofte qualyfyd
In takyng tyme or place as best may stand   140
Most easelye to dyspatche things cumyng in hand

114 *the*] *h* blotted, perhaps altered from *y*   115 *wurshypfull*] *p* written over another *f*
118 *he*] *h* altered from *y*   119 *paynes*] *s* altered   121 *sotts*] ²*s* blotted   *in*] tail added to *n*
122 *Cownterwaylth*] ²*w* altered, perhaps from *v*   123 *Feor*] *e* interlined above caret
127 *wyttles*] tail of *y* blotted   132 *horson*] long *s* begins with upstroke, not *e*
135 *beate*] possibly *beare*   *them*] tail added to *m*   136 *them*] tail added to *m*
137 *oporte[e]wnyte*] ¹*e* interlined above blotted *e* which is written over *w*   138 *placs*] *s*
perhaps altered

Wytt hathe provytyon alwey for releefe
To þvyde some remedy Agaynst myscheef
Wytty take bysynes as wytty wyll make yt
and as wytty beate wyttles / wyttles must take yt

————————————————————————————————————Iames

Tak yt howe ye lyst ye can make yt no les
But wytty have suche payne as my wordę wyttnes
ffor thowgh wytt for tyme sometyme may payne prevent
yet yn most tymes they[e]re foreseyde payne ys present   150
whych payne in the wytty wyttyly weyde
May match payne of the wyttles by ye fyrst leyde
and to the [secōd] second poynte / for dystemporate Ioyes
By havynge or hopynge of fancyes or toyes
In wyttyls[⟨.⟩] or wytty bothe tak I as one
ffor thowgh the thyngs that wytty have or hope on
Are yn some kynde of a cownt thyngs muche gretter
Then thyngs of the sotts Ioyings yet nowhyt better
                  t
Nor les payne bryngth ў passhyon / but endyfere[e]nt
To bothe / excepte wytty have the woors turment   160
Thyng yow a right good wytty havynge clerely
A thowsand pownd sodaynly gyvyn hym yerely   [Fol. 112a]
Who before that owre myght dyspend no peny
Nor tyll that owre never lokyd for eny
                      t
Myght not Ioy as muche ў soden recevyng
                                        ,
As Ioythe the sott reseyte of hys walsyngam rynge
And thereby be kepte from quyet sleepe a weke
as well as the rynge makethe the sotts sleepe to seeke

142 *provytyon*] [1]*o* mended   *alwey*] *e* written over a second *a*   147 *can*] tail added
to *n*   149 *thowgh*] [2]*h* written over *y*   *may*] interlined   150 *ys*] *s* has extra flourish
152 *ye*] after *e* an extra flourish, perhaps second *e* (for *yee*)   153 *dystemporate*] [1]*e* blotted
155 *wyttyls*[⟨.⟩]] *l* written over, and meant to replace [2]*y* (still visible); *s* perhaps written over *e*
156 *thowgh*] [2]*h* mended   *have*] *e* mended   *on*] *om* with last minim struck out   158 *Then*]
e ill shaped   159 *endyfere[e]nt*] character for *re* made [4]*e* superfluous   161 *clerely*] *re*
cramped   162 *thowsand*] *h* mended   164 *for*] *f* retraced   166 cross pencilled in
right margin

and in a soden leesyng that gyfte agayne
Myght not the wytty be presyd ẘ payne   170
as depe as the wyttles his ringe stolne or lost
And thowgh thys ensampyll chanse seelde when at most
yet sometyme yt happyth and dayly we see
That folke farr from wyttles passhynyd be
By Ioyfull hope of thyngs to them [tothe] lyk to hape
Or havyng / of things plesaunt late lyght in the lap
as muche to theyre vnrest for dystemprancy
As ye showde the wyttles restles formerly
And oft tyme for cawse consydryd and [v⟨.⟩y] weyde
As lyght / as yowr walsyngam rynge afore leyde   180
Wytt in wytty hathe seelyd suche perfecshyon
To bryng dysposyshyn full in abieckshyon
And the dyfferes of dysposyshyon ys such
Some wytts hope to lyttyll some wytts hope to muche
By whyche over muche I sey and sey must ye
That wytty and wyttles one in thys case be
And thus in bothe casys reasonyng cawse showthe
Cawse to [cōclude] conclewde that to the wytty growth
As muche payne As to the wyttles wherby
As good [be the] be wyttles as wytty say I.   190

                            —Iohn

That conclewcyon ys conclewdyd wysely
yowr pryme proposycyon dyd put presysely
Better to be wyttles then wytty and now
As good to be wyttles as wytty sey yow
But that [wytty] wytt / [wy] [wych] whych putth case in degre cōparatyve
And conclewdythe case in degre posytyve
Sall not in that case clayme degre sewperlatyve

                            —Iames

ye pas in this tawnt yowr prerogatyve   200

169 *in*] tail added to *n*   175 *them*] *m* added   179 *v[⟨.⟩]y*] letter smudged out
185 *whyche*] *yc* cramped   196 *[wy]*] interlined   198 *clayme*] *y* interlined above caret
200 *in*] tail added to *n*

25

But that wytt whyche bostythe ye full of his wynnyng
as thowgh[t] he knewe thende of thing at begynnyng
That wytt schall schow wyttles ympedy͞met
To be takyn wytty ẇ wytts excelent
I conclewde here not for thende but for the [d] myds
whyche / yf ye wyll here to end as reason byds   [FOL. 112b]
ye schall perceyve and also condysend
To grawnt me thanks then yn that I entende
yowr fall by feare handelynge to be ye more fayre
To set ye downe feately stayer after stayer   210
And so by a fayer fygewre of ynduckshyn
To bryng yor parte softe and fayer to dystrucksshyn
ffor where ye grawnt fully for owght yowr word℮ make
That as muche payne wytty as wyttles do[t] take
So from thys myds to the ende I schall prove
That most payne of twayne to the wyttles dothe move
ffor as I lode egally paynes of body
To wytty & wyttles lyke wyse [I] wyll I
Over lode the wyttyẇ payne of mynde
In mater as playne as can be a synde   220
whyche payne of mynde in mete mesewre to wey
ys more paynfull then payne of body [I] I seay

———————————————————————————————[Ia] Iohn

ye sey so and seyd so but so seyde not [I] I
Nor sey yt not yet but that seynge deny
and tyll saynge prove yor saynge more playnely
I wyll A sey to sey the contrary
I thynke paynes of body cowntyd in eche kynde
May compare ẇ all kynd℮ of paynes of mynde

206 *reason*] *a* interlined above caret   209 *fayre*] *y* written over *e*   212 *dystrucksshyn*]
²*s* blotted   214 *do[t]*] *t* altered before deletion   215 *thys*] *y* altered   *prove*] *v* written
over *w*   220 *can*] tail added to *n*   221 *payne*] inkblot, see-through from deletion in
l. 181   *in*] altered from *m* (the first letter of *mete* following), tail added   222 *seay*] *a*
doubtful

Iames   230

Yf ye assewrydly thynke as ye sey now
I thynke ye thynke as few men thynke but yow
howbeyt that beyng but an ynsydent
To pryncypall purpose presently ment
yet that excepshȳn took yow wyttyly
For had ye grawntyd that as ye schall schortly
Then forthw^t scholde owr pryncypall proses
[ffor A me] have concludyd in the parte that I profes
ffor a meane whervnto as mesewre may
Meet vnmesewrabull thyngę as who say   240
Ioyne in lyke [propo] proporshyn as may be ment
The meane laborer to the meane studyent
And ye schall anon fynde the stewdyents payne
More paynfull then the laborers labor playne

Iohn

The stewdyents payne ys ofte plesāutly myxt
In/felynge what frewte by his study ys fyxt

Iames

The [labors] laborers labor quyghthe that at a whyppe
In felynge the frewte hys wurkmanshyp   [FOL. 113a]
as muche delyght carters oft in carts neate trymd   251
as do studyents yn bokes wythe golde neate lymd
And as muche envy who may dreve hys cartebest
As a monge stewdyents who may seme lernd hyest
Wherby inwarde delyght to tolle forthe eche parte
Semthe me yndyfrent to/arte or to cart
And furder meane labor in most comon wyse
ys most parte hansome and holsome excersyse
That purgythe hewmors to mans lyfe and quycknes

---

232 *men*] e mended   238 *have*] interlined above deletion, which was eyeskip from l. 239
242 *studyent*] u flattened   245 *Iohn*] oh altered from *am*   250 *frewte hys*] *of* omitted?
251 *delyght*] g blotted   252 *neate*] a interlined above caret

[Also most kyndw]   260
Whyche study bredythe to mans dethe or sycknes
Also most kyndę of labor most comenly
strene most grose owtewarde partę of the body
Where study sparyng scholders fyngers and tose
To the hedde and hart dyrectly study gose
[perv] pervert ys yowr Iugment/yf ye iudge not playne
That les ys the parell and les ys the payne
The knockynge of knockylls whyche fyngers dothe strayne
Then dyggynge yn the hart or drying of the brayne
————————————————————————————[Ih] Iohn   270
ffor comun meane kyndę in bothe part[⟨.⟩]s now [l⟨.⟩y]de leyde
I se not but reason saythe as ye have seyde
————————————————————————————Iames

The labor of body and mynde thus compare
In what degrooe ye can devyse to declare
Betwene bothe / beynge not knyt/yn suche degre
But that thone from thother seperate may be
And that bothe labors yn Ioynynge ye A recte
as lyke yn degre as wytte may coniecte
and bothe ons serchyd serche schall make warantyse   280
yn labor of mynde the wurst payne dothe A ryse
————————————————————————————Iohn

Methynkthe I cowlde make yt other wyse A pere
Save I lacke tyme to dyla[y]te matter here
for tyme of reasonyng wolde be longe therin
And tyme of reasonynge must be/schort here in
Whyche weyde wͭ that this standthe [this standthe] but/Insydently

    260 *kyndw*] *w* for *Whyche* (in l. 261) after the deletion, and over ę   264 *scholders*] *c*
doubtful   266 *[perv]]* *v* written over *t* and obscured letter   268 *whyche*] [1]*h* interlined
above caret   269 *dyggynge*] [1]*g* mended   271 *meane*] [1]*e* blotted   *part[⟨.⟩]s*] blotted
letter above, perhaps *y*; *s* written over deletion   *[l⟨.⟩y]de*] second letter blotted, deletion not
completed   274 *body*] *dy* blotted   276 *Betwene*] [1]*e* written over *y*   277 *may*] *y*
blotted, possibly altered from *n*   282 *Iohn*] *Io* altered, perhaps from *Ia*   283 *pere*] [2]*e* added
285 *therin*] altered from *them* by interlining *r*, and adding another (superfluous?) minim to *m*

To owr present porpose pryncypally
I graunt to A gre As ye have defynde
Of labor of body and labor of mynde   290
That labor or payne of mynde ys the greter
And thys nowe grawntyd what be ye the better

——————————————————————————————————Iames

So muche the bettyr and yow so muche the wurs
that ye may now put yowr toong in yowr purs
for ony woorde indefens yowr toong schall tell
After thes my next woordę gyve eare and [mak] marke well   [Fol. 113b]
This labor of myndd whyche we now Agre
Above labor of body / we must decre
To Ioyne soole to the wytty for possybly   300
Cannot the wyttles take parte of that payne

——————————————————————————————————Iohn

Why

——————————————————————————————————Iames

How can he have payne by Imagynacyon
That lackythe all kynds of consyderatyon
and yn all sencys ys so yn sofycyent
That nowght can he thinke in owght ẙ may be ment
By ony meane to devyce ony selfe thinge
Nor devyse in thyng past present or cummynge   310
No more hathe he in mynde other payne or care
Then hathe other cocke my hors or gyll my mare
Thys cawse / ẘ wyttles payne of mynde dyspensys
But the wytty havynge all vytall sensys
hathe therby and Inwarde clocke/whyche marke who wyll

May oftymes go false / but yt never [to grown]d standythe styll
The plummets of that clocke come never to grownd
Imagynacyon ys watche and gothe so rownde
To whyche consyderacyon gyvythe so quycke eare
That in the wytty mynde / ye restles rest ys there   320
A small wytte may ges no wone wytte can deme
how ma[y]ny or how muche are theyre paynes extreme
Nor how many contrary kyndes in some one brest
yf ye perceyve thys tale ye se yt wytnest
Thre thyngs / of whyche the fyrst ys that the wyttles
Off labor or payne of mynde have reles
The seconde ys that the wytty have in vre
All paynes of mynde / and ẙ wytty dothe [p] ẙ [prpocere] proocvre
Thyrdly I glanset at payne of mynde A lewdyng
That payne to be most payne as in for conclewdyng   330
perceyve ye this

————————————————————————————————Iohn

ye and graw̄t yt trew to

————————————————————————————————Iames

Then must ye grawnt wytty to have most payne

————————————————————————————————Iohn

So I do

————————————————————————————————Iames

yf wytty have most payne of tweyne ye must say
Better to be wyttles then wytty   340

————————————————————————————————Iohn

Nay

————————————————————————————————Iames

I say yes

316 *standythe*] interlined above caret over deletion, which was eyeskip from l. 317   *styll*]
added slightly below line: all these corrections in an ink of a different colour   317 *to grownd*]
added above caret   322 *theyre*] *y* interlined above caret   324 *thys*] *h* altered from *y*
327 *seconde*] *o* written over *d*   328 *[prpocere]*] ^{2}*p* interlined above *r* and deleted   *proocvre*]
c doubtful   329 *at*] possibly *ar*   332 *Iohn*] *I* blotted   334 *Iames*] *I* retraced
335 *grawnt*] *n* flattened   336 *Iohn*] *h* altered from *y*   339 *yf*] *f* mended

—————————————————————————————————Iohn

I say nay and wyll so envey   [FOL. 114a]
That I wyll holde ye to wagge another w[a]ey
as I grawnt wytty of [have most plesewre] twayne most payne/endewre
So wyll I prove wytty to have most plesewre
whych plesewre schall bothe drowne the wyttys payne   350
and the plesewer yn whyche the wyttles remayne

—————————————————————————————————Iames

Thys þomyse wyll hardly bryng good paymēt
ffor yt ys a strange kynde of argewmēt
To þve hym in most plesewre who hathe most payne
Or hym yn least payne who least plesewre dothe sustayne

—————————————————————————————————Iohn

Let vs reason all plesewrs on bothe sydes
And then let that syde have best that best þvydes

—————————————————————————————————Iames   360

All plesewrs on bothe sydes that were A thynge
To make vs make ende to morow mornyg

—————————————————————————————————Iohn

A⟨.⟩/ now the best parte of my parte cumth on
ye make marvelus hast / ye wolde fayne be gone

—————————————————————————————————Iames

Right now yowr self cowld wey in rightwytty so[⟨.⟩]rt
That resonyng here now of reason must beschort

—————————————————————————————————Iohn

yt schalbe schort Inowgh yf ye take a [wey] wey   370
All that parte that for my part effeckte dothe ley

—————————————————————————————————Iames

I wyll nother take A wey all nor take all

---

347 *to*] interlined, and ill formed   *w[a]ey*] *e* interlined above deletion   348 *of*] perhaps altered from *to*; *twayne most payne* interlined above deletion with caret deleted; words were eyeskip from the end of l. 349   349 *plesewre*] *es* blotted   350 *drowne*] *r* mended 364 ²*parte*] *e* extended over *cumth*   367 *in*] tail added to *n*   *so[⟨.⟩]rt*] *r* interlined above blotted letter   368 *reason*] *ea* altered   373 *wey*] *e* altered

But for a meane betwene bothe / my self streyght schall
Alege / n[e]ot plesewrs all I sey but such one
As over weythe other plesewrs evry chone
Whyche plesewrs where yt in fyne dothe not remayne
All plesewrs in all partts ar plesewrs but vayne
Of whyche one plesewre the wyttles ar sewre evyr
And of that plesewre wytty are sewre nevyr   380

———————————————————————————————————————Iohn

What plesewre ys that

———————————————————————————————————————Iames

Plesewre of salvashyon
I thyn[g]ke yowr selfe wyll affyrme affyrmashyon
That from owrr forfathers syn orygynall
Babtym sealythe vs all A quyttās generall
and faythe of ynfants whyle they Infants Abyde
In faythe of parents [g]for the churche ys supplyde
wherby tyll wytt take roote of dysernygne   390
and betwene good & yll geve perfyght warnynge
[whe⟨.⟩r] where ever Innosents Innosensy dyspewte
for thowghts woorddᵉ or dedes god dothe none yll ympewte
Wher god gyvythe no dysnernyng god takethe none acownte   [FOL. 114b]
In whyche case of a cownt the sot dothe amownt
ffor no more [dyservythe] dysernythe the sott at yeres thre score
Then thynosent borne wͭ in yeres thre before
This schort sayng yf ye yn mynde revolve
Then schall thys longe debate [foothwͭ] forthwͭ dysolve

———————————————————————————————————————Iohn   400

Syr I grawnt sottᵉ schall be savyd as ye tell
And safe schall wytty be to yf they do well

374 *streyght*] *y* altered   375 *n[e]ot*] *o* interlined with caret above blotted *e*   *plesewrs*]
²*e* blotted   378 *partts*] ¹*t* interlined, ²*t* blotted   379 *evyr*] *y* altered from *e*
383 *Iames*] *a* altered   385 *affyrmashyon*] *h* altered from *y*   386 *owrr*] ¹*r* interlined
387 cross pencilled in left margin   389 *In*] tail added to *n*   391 *betwene*] ¹*e* altered
from *y*   392 *ever*] ²*e* altered from *y*   393 *woorddᵉ*] ¹*o* interlined   *ympewte*] *ew* altered
395 *case*] *e* mended   399 *[foothwͭ]*] ²*o* interlined

——————————————————————————————————Iames

Yff they do well that yf altryth muche lo
Theffeckte of my sentens to wyttles

——————————————————————————————————Iohn

How so

——————————————————————————————————Iames

That yf leyde for the wytty purporthe a dowte
But all dowtes in the wyttles are scrapte clene owte   410
Sans dowte the wyttles ys sewer of salvashyon
Wherby / to conclewde thys comynycashyon
Make wytty sewer of all plesewrs can be leyde
dowtyng lacke of none but thys one plesewre last seyde
And of all plesewrs wyttles to [lacke] have none
Savynge he standthe in sewrte of this one
ys not the sewrte of thys one muche bettyr
then of the rest thowgh the nomber be grettyr

——————————————————————————————————Iohn

Yes   420

——————————————————————————————————Iames

Lyke as a goose can say nothynge but hys
So hathe he now nothynge nothynge to say but yes
and in affyrmyng my saynge he saythe thys
In whyche he grawtthe his partt not partly a mys
But all a mys as who saythe in all placys
The sum wherof in bothe partes standthe in thre casys
Off w^che thre thargewment of the fyrst was thus
In laboryvs payne of body to dyscus
who soferythe more the wytty or the sott   430
yn whyche / by both[y]e assents / we knyt thys knott
That as muche payne of body in effeckte/hathe ye one

409 *the*] *h* altered   412 *conclewde*] *w* interlined above caret   414 *seyde*] [1]*e* altered
415 *have*] *v* blotted   425 *partt*] [2]*t* added   427 *partes*] *e* written over *s* and another
s added   431 *both[y]e*] *y* has a flourish; deletion doubtful

33

As thother / conclewdyng thus ffarre there vppon
As good to be wyttles as wytty and then
We argewde labor or payne of mynde in men
Wherin I dryvyng hym to grawnt payne of mynde
More then payne or labor bodyly defynde
In [the] the seconde case[⟨.⟩] I payne of mynde provyng
To wytty and not to wyttles to be movyng
Drave hym to grawnt furder that by ẙ payne   440
[B⟨.⟩t better]
Better ẘowte wytt then ẘ wytt to remayne
Now in thys thyrde case where ye made A bragge
By plesewrs in the wytty to holde me wagge   [FOL. 115a]
And plesewrs of the wyttles to over whelme
I stamynge in ẘ hym stacke so to the helme
That [is] hys parte fynally to shypwracke ys browght
The sewrte of all plesewrs in this worlde wrowght
Matche not the sew[e]rte of plesewre eternall
And thestate[s] of sotts have none acownt so carrnall   450
That god ympewtthe any yll to them I say
and the wyttyse acownt awgmenthe evry day
And thawdytors wytt who schall take thacownt so clere
he [forgeth] forgethe not wone worde in a thowsand yere
what nede mo woordę I thynke the least wytt here
Sethe thes thre casys on my syde so a pere
That in the two fyrst casys temporally
And in this thyrd and last case spyrytewally
Ys sene fully I may conclewde fynally
Better to be wyttles then to be wytty   460

————————————————————————————Iohn

So sey I now to by owr blyssyd lady

436 *hym*] *y* altered   *mynde*] *e* added   438 *case[⟨.⟩]*] deleted letter may be virgule
442 *Better*] *r* blotted   499 *sew[e]rte*] deletion doubtful   *eternall*] curl over ²*e*
450 *carrnall*] ¹*r* interlined   452 *evry*] *v* altered   453 *thawdytors*] *w* altered
454 *[forgeth]*] *e* blotted   457 *fyrst*] *f* perhaps *ff*

I gyve vppe my part and take yor part playnly
Off wytty and wyttles I wysche now rather
That my chylde may have A foole to hys father
The pythe of yowr conclewsyons be all so pewre
That better be a foole then A wyse man sewre
———————————————————————————————Ierome

Not so / all thowgh yowr fancy do so surmyse
not better for man to be wytles then wyse   470
Nor so good to be wyttles As wytty nother
Thus ys yowr wytt dysseyvyd in other
———————————————————————————————Iohn

Why / what dyffrens betwene wyse and [wytty] wytty
———————————————————————————————Ierome

As muche sometyme as betwene wysdom and folly
———————————————————————————————Iohn

Man can in nowyse be wyse w^t owte/wytt
———————————————————————————————Ierome

No / and man may have gret wytt and wysdom nowhyt   480
[Whyt] wytt ys the wurker of all perseyvyng
and indyferet to good or yll wurkyng
And as muche wytt may be in thynge of most yll
As in the best thyngys wytt can aspyre vntyll
In vertu or vyse I meane and wytt hathe receyght
Off none yll / where wytt vppon [wysdon] wysdom dothe weyght
Wysdome governth wytt alweay vertu to vse   [FOL. 115b]
and all kynds of vyce alway to refewse
Thus ys wysdom in good parte takyn alweyse
And gydythe wytt in all thynge beynge thyngs of preyse   490
Thus thowgh ye must (as ye nede not) graunt his grownd

_____

467 *then*] *e* mended   471 *nother*] *h* altered from *y*   474 *[wytty]*] ²*y* altered
476 *betwene*] *et* smudged   480 *nowhyt*] *yt* mended   484 *thyngys*] ²*y* partly obscured
by *s*, and possibly deleted   *can*] extra minim deleted   485 *In*] tail added to *n*
486 *wysdom*] interlined above deletion, with caret   487 *governth*] *er* cramped   *alweay*] *e*
interlined with caret; *a* retraced   489 *alweyse*] *l* altered   490 *in*] tail added to *n*

35

Whyche ys / better wyttles then wytty to be fownd
yet as muche as wysdom above wytt/schowth
so muche grawntyd ye hym more then of nede growthe
———————————————————————————————Iames

Thys ys some yownge schooleman A freshe [commor] comonar
harde ye the pryncypyll that plantyd thys Iar
———————————————————————————————Ierome

I harde all
———————————————————————————————Iames   500

and dothe not all on my syde fall
———————————————————————————————Ierome

No / yf ye had resonyd as I schall
———————————————————————————————Iames

Yf ye as ye say have harde all here sayde
And ẙ ye that saying have so wydely wayd
To way my parte wurst herein in conclewsyon
Then ar ye wyttles ẙ we towe talkt on
But babyll yoᴿ wyll / thys wyll I byde vppon
Better be sott somer then sage salamon   510
———————————————————————————————Ierome

geve ye sentens or ye here what I cane say
Loo how wyll carythe hym and hys wytte Away
———————————————————————————————Iohn

Syr yf ye harde all in my part how say ye ,
what dyd I graunt hym to farre schow I py ye
———————————————————————————————Ierome

All that ys grauntyd welnye
———————————————————————————————Iohn

Nay I trow   520

    494 *nede*] [1]*e* altered   497 *pryncypyll*] [3]*y* altered from *a*   501 *dothe*] *d* altered from *n*
503 *ye*] *y* altered from *h*   *resonyd*] *d* altered   504 *Iames*] *a* altered, probably from *e*
506 *saying*] *i* interlined above caret   510 cross pencilled in left margin   *salamon*] [2]*a*
altered from *o*   511 *Ierome*] *o* altered   512 *cane*] tail added to *n*

—————————————————————————————————Ierome

Ye schall when we have done not trow but know
for entre wherto I p̓y ye answere me
A questyon or twayne or mo yf nede be
And fyrst vnto thys answere as ye can
Whether wolde ye be A resonable man
or an vnresonabyll beast

—————————————————————————————————Iohn

By and sell
I wolde be the symplest man betwene hevyn and hell   530
rather then the best beast y̔ ever was bred

—————————————————————————————————Ierome

Then yf ye of one of the twayne must be sped
Ye woolde be a maltman / ye a myller
Rather then a mylhorse

—————————————————————————   ——————Iohn

                        Iohn   [FOL. 116a]
Be ye my well wyller

—————————————————————————————————Ierome

Ye   540

—————————————————————————————————Iohn

Speke no more of thys then what man fye
I wold not be a beast for all this worlde / I
w[h]ere yt for nowght ells but for this lyfe pres̄et

—————————————————————————————————Ierome

The tyme of this lyfe in dede I meane and ment
but tell me why by yoͬ faythe evyn playnely
Ye wyl/not change estate w̔ the myll horse

---

522 *when*] h altered from *e*   523 *entre*] [2]*e* added to the end of the character for *re*
527 *an*] tail added to *n*   536 *Iohn*] blot before *I*   537 *Iohn*] cropped at top of page
540 *Ye*] *e* altered   543 *beast*] *a* interlined   544 *lyfe*] *f* altered   545 *Ierome*] [1]*e*
altered, possibly from *o*   547 *faythe*] curl before *t*, perhaps tail from *y*

37

───Iohn

Why / there be whyse and wherforrse I thyngke A thowsand   550
In cownt of two kynds of [thyngks] things cumyng in hande
Sensybyll plesewre / and sensybyll payne
and fyrst for payne sustaynyd in thes twayne
begyn ẘ the myll hors whom ye put for/prefe
Or ony lyke beast sustaynyge the lyke grefe
And or I wolde take the payne the poore beasts take
I wolde eche day be twygde and tyde [ast] to a stake
Carying fro the myll carying to the myll
Drowyng in the myll poore Iade he Ietthe styll
Ambyll he / trot he / go he a foote pase   560
Walope he / galop he / racke he in trase
Yf hys pase please not be yt softe or faster
The spures or whypp schalbe [h] hys pay master
W[h]ere not a man trow ye in plesaunt case
Wᵗ a beast in thys case to change case or plase
No man excepte some few so ynfortewnate
That they be owt of thacownt of mans estate
That wolde agre to leve to change paynes I trow
Wythe beasts payne beynge such as all men know
Now to speke of plesewre in thes twayne asynde   570
the beaste to [compayrre] c̄opare ys to far behynde
plesewr dyscussybyll in thes thus dothe fall
The beast in effecte hathe none the man hathe all
The resonabyll manns Imagynashyon
Ioynde ẘ resonabyll consyderatyon
Bryngthe man muche plesewre in consyder̄yg

─────

550 *Why*] belongs metrically at the end of l. 548   *wherforrse*] ³*r* interlined   551 *hande*]
extra flourish after *d*, perhaps *dd*   552 *plesewre*] ¹*e* altered   554 *prefe*] ²*e* altered
555 *ony*] *o* mended   *grefe*] *f* mended   556 *beasts*] *a* altered from *s*   561 ³*he*] *e* mended
562 *please*] *ea* cramped   570 *twayne*] *y* interlined above caret   571 *[compayrre]*] ²*r*
interlined   574 *Imagynashyon*] *hy* mended and blotted

38

The plesaut proporte of eche plesaunt thynge
possesyd to mans behofe at comandynge
beasts have thyngs of nede but no furder pleasynge
Syns man hathe/releefe for all nesessyte   580
As well as beast and above beaste comodyte
Of plesewrs plantyd for mans recreatyon
In the hyest kynd to mans contentatyon
Whereby plesewre in effecte betwene thes twayne   [Fol. 116b]
Showthe thus / man hathe all / beast hathe none & more payne
hathe beast [the] then resonabyll man / by thes bothe
[C] change fro man to beast who wyll / I wolde be lothe

                 Ierome

Ye have yn my myndde thys [⟨.⟩] right well defynde
and for cawse kepe yt well a [wyl] while yn yowr/mynde 590
set we a oyde man and beasts symvlytewde
And full dysposytyon in bothe ao we vewde
what thyng dysposythe most the varyete
Betwene man and beast

               [Iames] Iohn

Reson in man perde

                 Ierome

That man who of reason ys as destytute
As a beast ys / what dyffrens schall we dyspewte

                 Iohn 600

Small in this case excepte yt[⟨.⟩] be this one
The sott hathe a resonabyll sowle beasts have none

                 Ierome

What helpyth/the wytt of the sowle in the sott
Syns the body ys suche yt vsythe yt not
where ympotensy planthe suche ympedyments

583 *In*] *I* blotted 584 *plesewre*] ³*e* mended 585 *none*] *e* altered 587 *change*] *e*
altered and blotted 590 *[wyl]*] another letter interlined above *y* and abandoned
592 *dysposytyon*] *t* altered, partly obscured by tail from *n* in *man* in l. 591 593 *the*] *th* blotted
598 *reason*] *a* interlined above caret 601 *yt[⟨.⟩] be*] cancelled letter possibly ampersand
606 *ympedyments*] ²*m* flattened to a dash

That vse of sensys are voyde to all yntents
for vse of reason / so that for vse of wytt
They ar as beasts [wyttles] wyttles vsyng wytt nowhyt
In man thus wytles and thunresonabyll beaste   610
I se small dyffrens for thys lyfe at leaste
———Iohn

I [grãwt] grawnt / the wyttles and the beast thus as one
———Ierome

Then schall thes beasts wyttles man and mylhors draw on
Bothe [one] yn one yoke / for thynke yow the nomber
Standthe as somer dothe all day yn slomber
Nay somer ys a sot foole for a kynge
But sots in ma[y]ny other mens howsyng
beare water beare woodde and do yn drugery   620
In kychyn cole howse & in the norsery
And dayly for fawtes whyche they cannot refrayne
Evyn lyke the myll hors they be whyppyd amayne
Other fooles that labor not have other conseyts
vppon thydyll foole the flocke euer more weytes
They tos hym / they turne hym he is Iobd & Iolde
Whyth frettyng and fewmyng as ye a fore tolde
Excepte mayster somer of sotts not the best
but the myllhors may compare w̃ hym for rest
The for plesewr conceyvyng or [r] receyvynge   630
The wyttles and mylhors are bothe as one thyng
Yowr last tale and thys tale to gether conferd   [FOL. 117a]
by matter of/bothe let yoᵣ answere be harde
Whether ye/wolde be a man rosonabyll
Or vnresonabyll / and excepte ye fabyll
Thys answere schall schow playne & vndowtydly

607 *are*] *e* added   623 *whyppyd*] *h* altered, perhaps from *y*   626 ¹*hym*] *h* altered
628 cross pencilled in left margin   *Excepte*] ²*e* doubtful   630 *[r] receyvynge*] *r* deleted
for *re* character   632 *Yowr*] *Y* possibly *y*   633 *yoʳ*] extra flourish after *r*
634 *ye*] *e* altered   636 *answere*] *w* altered and ¹*e* interlined above caret

whether ye wolde be wyttles or wytty

——Iohn

In good faythe I take thys conclewcyon so full
That I may geve over and evyn so I wull   640
for thys lyfe

——Ierome

well then for the lyfe to come
few woords where reason ys may [⟨.⟩] knyt vppe the sům
Concernyng plesewre after thys lyfe present
By whyche he and yow dyssolvyd argewment
bothe parts by bothe partyse were so endyd
that yo͏ʳ part full faynt⟨.⟩ly ye defendyd
Thowgh the mere meryte of owr redemtyon
Stande In cristys passyon yet in exemsyon   650
therof / schall we stand / by gods Iustyce / excepte
havynge tyme and wytt / hys comandments be kept
And who in whyche dothe most dylygently
plant ymps of good woorcks gyvyn by god chefely
most hyly of god schall he have rewarde

——Iohn

How prove ye that

——Ierome

By scrypture / have in regarde
Cryst in the gospell of Iohn dothe thys declare   660
In the howse of my father sayth crist ther/are
Dyvers and ma[y]ny mantyons that ys to say
As thexposytyon of saynt Awstyne dothe/way
There are in [ev] hevyn dyvers degrees of glory
To be [reyv] [re] receyvyd of men A cordyngly
Eche man as he vsythe gods gyfts of grace
So schall/he have in hevyn hys degre or place
but marke thys chefe grownd the sům of scrypture saythe

652 *wytt*] another letter begun after ²t but cancelled at once   653 *who*] w has false start, and is cramped   655 *of*] f altered from r   657 *How*] H altered   658 *Ierome*] ¹e altered from o   659 *have*] v perhaps altered   661 *In*] tail added to n

41

We must walke w̌ thes gyfts in the pathe of faythe
In whyche walke who wurkthe most in gods comandment 670
he schall have most & [sent] seynt powle schowthe lyke entent
As one starre dyfferthe from an other in schynynge
so the resurrectyon of the ded whyche lyke thynge
Aperthe in other placys of scrypture

───────────────────────────────────Iohn

I grawnt/and what than

───────────────────────────────────Ierome

       Ierome   [FOL. 117b]
That what cumth streyght in vre
Syns he/that vsythe gods gyfts best schall have best 680
and he next who dothe next and so forthe the rest
and that the wytty do dayly wurke or may
and the wyttles nowght wurkythe by no way
so that hys rewarde may cõpare in degre
yf wytty have thys A vantage thynkythe me
The wyse wyttyse place wysche I desyrusly
Rather then place of the wyttles

───────────────────────────────────Iohn

So do I
Yff wysche wolde wyn yt but where yᵉ sot ys sewre 690
The wytty standthe in hasardous adventewre
To lees all/and so in fyne fayre and well
In sted of way to hevyn to take the waye to hell
In wurks comandyd who in faythe walkthe not
by gods Iustyce he hathe damnatyon in lott
and what other folks fele I can not tell
but suche frayle falls fele I in my selfe to dwell
and by them to lees hevyn I am so a drad

  670 *In*] tail added to *n*   *who*] *h* altered from *y*   676 *and*] interlined above caret
679 *streyght*] ¹*t* added and blotted   *in vre*] below line; practice marks in ink in right margin
682 *wurke*] *k* blotted   683 *wurkythe*] *wu* altered   685 *thynkythe*] ¹*h* altered
688 *Iohn*] *h* blotted   691 *hasardous*] *o* altered   693 *In*] tail added to *n*   696 *folks*]
perhaps *folkes*   698 *hevyn*] *e* blotted   *drad*] *a* altered from *e*

The sotts sewrte of least Ioy there wolde god I hadde
An olde proverb makythe ẘ thys whyche I take good   700
Better one byrde in hand then [then] ten in the wood

———————————————————————————————————————Ierome

What yf of the ten byrds in the woode eche one
were as good as that one in yo͛ hand alone
and that ye myght cache them all ten yf ye wolde
Wolde ye not leve one byrde for the ten now tolde

———————————————————————————————————————Iohn

yes

———————————————————————————————————————Ierome

wolde ye not havynge helpe take resonabyll payne   710
for thencres of ten byrds for one in gayne

———————————————————————————————————————Iohn

yes

———————————————————————————————————————Ierome

Then in gods name feare not let fle thys one
ye schall I trust catche thes ten byrds evry chone
yowr fleshly frayle falls are suche ẙ ye drede
As muche as hope / in havynge hevynly mede
by whyche [drede] dred sewrte of Ioyes there y͛ most small
Wysche ye rather then byd venture to have Ioyes all   720
and the soner by this ye chose thys I deme
The least Ioy there ys more then man can/esteme
But now to remove thys [bo] blocke yo͛ grett drede   [FOL. 118a]
we have a lever that removethe drede ẘ spede
god sofether but not wylthe ony man to syne
Nor god wylthe no synners dethe but he be yn
suche endles males ẙ hys fynall estate
In lacke of penytens make hym selfe reprobate

700 *An*] *A* altered from *a*   701 cross pencilled in left margin   *[then]*] *n* half formed
and then abandoned   705 *them*] *h* written over *y*   707 *Iohn*] *I* mended   710 *resonabyll*]
e added to *r*   717 *suche*] *h* altered, perhaps as *e* was added   722 *can*] tail added to *n*
724 *removethe*] ¹*e* added clumsily   725 cross pencilled in left margin   728 *In*] tail
added to *n*

43

In tyme of this lyfe at eche penytent call
[ffrom the p] Owrr marcyfull maker remytthe synns all   730
ffrom the perpetewall peyne infernall
what [ere] ever they be from least to most carnall
by whyche goodnes of god we are set in hopes chayer
Not to brede presumpsyon but to banyshe dyspayre
The grace of god alw[⟨.⟩]ey to grace alewrthe man
And when man wyll call for g̃ce of g̃ce asewrthe man
To assyst man gods comandments to fulfyll
At all tymes yf man cast owte yll wyllynge wyll
Nowe syns the crystyane that wurkythe most in faythe
schall have most in rewarde as the scrypture saythe   740
and y̍ gods g̃ce by [g⟨.⟩e] g̃ce cald for wyll asyst
Mans wyll to wurke well alwey when man lyst
And at instant of dew ordryd penytenᵃ
Man hathe gods mercy of all former offens
Whyche schowthe for mercy man ys not more gredy
To ax then god to grawnt mercy ys redy
Thys sene what schow yow to mayntayne the feare
Whyche ye towarde desperatyon were in whyle eare

———————————————————————————————Iohn

What schow I / nay the schow of/that frare ys extyngkt   750
Evyn by thys praty tale thus pythyly lynkt
syns god[to] to the most faythfull wurker gyvythe most
And to make man wurke muche god hasthe as in post
And where man hathe not wrowght / at contrytyon
god grawnthe man of damnatyon remytyon
makynge man sewre of frewte of crystys passyon

729 *In*] tail added to *n*   730 *Owrr*] [1]*r* interlined; the word is written over the smudge
used to delete the false start, caused by eyeskip to l. 731   *remytthe*] *h* written over *y*
732 *[ere]*] [2]*e* interlined   733 *whyche*] *wh* altered   *goodnes*] *d* altered, perhaps *dd* intended
735 *of*] *f* blotted   *alw[⟨.⟩]ey*] *e* interlined above deletion with caret   737 *fulfyll*] [2]*f* altered
from *l*   738 *owte*] *e* added   740 *rewarde*] [1]*e* added, to clarify *re* character
743 *And*] *n* altered   *instant*] [2]*t* altered from *c*   744 *offens*] *s* blotted   747 *feare*] [2]*e*
added, to clarify *re* character   748 *were*] [2]*e* added   750 [1]*schow* and [2]*schow*] *c* doubtful
754 *contrytyon*] [2]*t* altered   756 *sewre*] [1]*e* added

Excepte mans wylfull wyll / mar all good fascyon
by this I drede god as [standthe] standthe w̃ love & hope
but no desperate drede dothe my hart now grope

—————————————————————————————Ierome   760

Ten byrds in the wood or one in hande alone
Whych chose ye now

—————————————————————————————Iohn

        Iohn   [FOL. 118b]
I wyll not change ten for one
syns the byrder wyl helpe me to tak them all
As sewre to myne vse as the one byrde cowld fall

—————————————————————————————Ierome

Well for conclewsyon syns ye sowndly se
That wytty have plesewre here in more degre   770
Then wytles and also wytty wyse se ye
In hevyn by scrypture in lyer Ioyce be
then the wyttles / yow seyng thys clerely
Whether wold ye now be wyttles or wytty

—————————————————————————————Iohn

Wytty / and the more wytty am I for yow
Of whych hartyly I thanke yow and now
Where my mate my lords sayde that ys gone
better be sot somer then sage salamon
[I] In for sakynge that I woolde now rather be   780
Sage saloman then sot somer I assewre ye

—————————————————————————————Ierome

As ye schow wyt in change of former mynde
beyng [fro] now from wytles to wytty enclynde
so aply yoᵣ wytt in what/wytt schall devyse

758 *[standthe]*] *d* added   764 *Iohn*] tail added to *n*   769 *conclewsyon*] *e* perhaps
altered   772 *In*] tail added to *n*   773–5 blots on text and in margin   777 *hartyly*]
¹*y* altered   779 cross pencilled in left margin   780 *In*] tail added to *n*   *woolde*] ²o
interlined above caret   783 *in*] tail added to *n*

As in good vse of wytt by grace ye may ryse
To be bothe wytty and wyttyly wyse
In governās of gods gyfts in suche syse
as wysdom Alw[a]ey gydyth wherby [this] thys schall fall
gods gyfts to gods glory bothe ye may vse and schall   790

Thes woords of cowncell in whyche I now wadyd
to hym whom I tolde them I onely A syne
I am by all cyrcumstance full perswadyd
this sort beyng sortyd in sort [this] thus fyne
nede none exortatyon or at least not myne
Thys sort have not onely by [natur] natewre hys wytt
but also by grace lyke wysdom Ioynde to [h] yt

    Thes thre stave next folowyng in the
    Kyngs Absens / are voyde

And/as in them therby gods gyfts schyne most man   [FOL. 119a]
so stand ther affayres wherby they so schyne schall   801
yf the glos of gods schyne not bryght eche way
In them who havyng A realme in governall
set forthe theyre governans to gods glory all
Charytably aydynge subiects in eche kynde
The schynyng of gods gyfts wheer[⟨.⟩] schall we then fynde

And of this hye sort the hy hed most excelēt
ys owr most loved and drade supreme soferayne
The schynynge of whose most excellent [⟨.⟩] talent
ymployde to gods glory Above all the trayne   810
syns wytt wantyth here recytall to retayne

788 *In*] tail added to *n*   *gyfts*] *t* indistinct   789 *Alw[a]ey*] *e* interlined above deletion [*this*]] scribe attempted to change *i* to *y*, mistakenly put tail on *h*, and then deleted the word 792 *them*] *he* altered and blotted   797 *wysdom*] *m* altered from *n*   800 *in*] pen trail above *n*   *gyfts*] *t* indistinct   *most*] *st* blotted, *s* altered   *man*] distinct *n*, but dotted as if for *y* 805 *Charytably*] ²*y* retraced   806 *wheer[⟨.⟩]*] *r* interlined above deletion with caret; ²*e* possibly *a*   807 *most*] *m* altered from *no*   809 *of*] possibly *ofe*

And that all hys faythfull fele ye frewte of hys fame
Of corse I pray pardon in passyng the same

[praynge]

Prayng that pryns whome owr pryns hys grett grace gave
To grawnt/hym longe lengthe of encres in estate
At full fyne wherof hys most [t]hy gyfts to have
by his most faythfull vse rewarde in suche rate
as ys promysyd in scrypture alegyd late
The Ioyes / not all onely in estymabyll   820
But more the degre of Ioyes incomparabyll

Contynewans wherof w̌ frewtfull encrese
I/hartyly wysche for encrese of rewarde
As scrypture A legyd [layte]/late doth wytnes
The wytty wyse wurker to be prefarde
A bove thydyll [sot]/sot / and ye to regarde
Eche man hym selfe so to aply in thys
As ye all may obtayne the hye degre of blys

amen qd Iohn heywod

[BLANK]   [FOL. 119b]

813 *corse*] *e* added   814 *[praynge]*] smudged out, beneath oblique line, presumably to maintain consistent spacing between stanzas   819 *alegyd*] *d* altered   822–8 in the final stanza the handwriting is noticeably larger   822 *frewtfull*] ^{2}*f* altered from *e*   823 *I*] portion of tail deleted   *of*] possibly *ofe*; uncertain because of a hole in the page   825 *wyse*] *e* added   *prefarde*] *a* blotted, perhaps altered from *e*   826 *[sot]*] *o* altered   829 *qd*] ?*qh*; letters formed unusually, or conflated; lines drawn around three sides of subscription

LIKE WILL TO LIKE
BY
ULPIAN FULWELL
1568

INTRODUCTION

THE TEXT

LIKE WILL TO LIKE was entered in the Stationers' Register in about September 1568:

Rₑ of Iohn alde for his lycense for prynting of a play lyke Wyll to lyke qᵈ the Devell to the Collyer   iiijᵈ[1]

The play survives in three sixteenth-century quarto editions. The first, Q1, was printed by John Allde, and is dated 1568 on the title-page. The second, an undated edition, Q2, was also printed by Allde. Greg suggested that because Q1 bears a date it must be the earlier of the two editions, and no evidence has been put forward to contradict this.[2] The third edition, Q3, was printed in 1587 by John Allde's son, Edward, in the same Long Shop adjoining St Mildred's Church in the Poultry.[3] The unique copy of Q1 is in the Bodleian Library: this was Edmond Malone's own copy, and it contains annotations in his hand. The Folger Shakespeare Library owns the unique copy of Q2. The three known copies of Q3 are in the British Library, the Huntington Library, and the Elizabethan Club, Yale University.

All three quartos collate A–E⁴, F², and are black letter. Q1 and Q2 have a smaller font for stage directions, songs and part of the title-page, and roman for Latin phrases (including 'Exit', 'Exeunt', and 'Intrat') and a few proper names. In Q3 most of the title-page, the stage-directions, and speech-headings are set in roman. The names of speakers, which are in the outer margins, are heavily cropped in the surviving copies of Q1 and Q2. A significant amount of damage has also been done to the top lines of Q1 by cropping.[4] In Q2 there

---

[1] Greg, *Bibliography*, i. 4 and pp. xxi–xxii.

[2] Q1, Q2, and Q3 are STC 11473, 11473.5, 11474. The title-page of Q2 is reproduced as Plate 3 (Q2 pages are shown full-size in the plates).

[3] John Allde was apprenticed to Richard Kele and gained his freedom in 1555. He used his former master's shop, as noted in the imprint. He is known to have printed over fifty books between 1562 and 1582. There were several texts of plays among them: *Nice Wanton* (Q2, [1565?]); *Like Will to Like* (1568); *The Four PP* (Q3, 1569); *Cambises* [1570?]; *Jack Juggler* (Q3, [c.1570]); and *Enough is as Good as a Feast* [1570?]. Edward Allde printed from about 1584, and moved from the shop in 1588.

[4] There are variations in the height and breadth of pages in both copies. The maximum measurements are: Q1, 173 × 120 mm.; Q2, 174 × 128 mm. The watermark in Q1 is a jug with the letters 'NB' (or 'NR') on the belly. The jug is not clear enough for comparison with Heawood or Briquet watermarks. As might be expected in a quarto, the upper portion of the jug appears on A4, B4, C4, and D4, and the lower portion on A1, B1, C1, and D1. A portion of the jug appears on E1, but not elsewhere in gathering E. There is no watermark visible in F1 and F2. The watermark in Q2 is barely discernible, but it is certainly smaller than the one in Q1, and different in design.

51

are no running heads, and there is no sign of them in what remains of Q1. A five-line stave of music appears on D4r in both Q1 and Q2: Q3 omits this.

The text of Q1 was printed thirty-four lines to the page, including the lines for the signatures and catchwords. What evidence there is suggests that it was set by a single compositor. Spelling patterns point to one individual (final 'e' on 'muche', 'suche', 'iche', and 'whiche', with no exceptions), as does the consistent use of ligatured letters in small type ('ss', 'oo', 'st', 'fi', 'ct', and 'si'). The use of the letters 'ee' for 'hee', 'wee', 'heer', and 'bee' is evenly distributed throughout the text, although the conventional spellings 'he', 'we', 'here', and 'be' appear with about the same frequency. The evidence of the punctuation is inconclusive. Colons, for example, are used with noticeable regularity at the end of the first line of couplets, and at the end of the second line of quatrains. This may, however, be a sign of Allde's house style (see below).

There are some indications that Q2 was set from Q1, although how much later it is impossible to say. Q2 follows the lineation of Q1 almost exactly. There are no additional or omitted lines, and the few changes of wording appear to come from the printing house. Most of these were intended as improvements to meaning, or in spacing. There were two exceptions. (*a*) Because the compositor of Q2 moved the pilcrows at the beginnings of speeches into the body of the text, he was forced to make space to the right. In doing so he allowed lines to run over, and was obliged to re-line and condense some of the marginal stage directions.[5] (*b*) On two occasions he also repositioned lines from their place, in Q1, at the bottom of a page to a new place at the top of the next. In one instance, the anomalous division of the stanza of a song in Q1 (the first line on D3v and the other four on D4r, ll. 946 and 947–50), in contrast with its more regular setting in Q2, suggests that Greg's view about the sequence of the quartos was probably correct (see Plate 6). There was probably a comparable attempt at improvement in the Q2 setting of l. 1307, which appears at the head of F1v instead of, as in Q1, the foot of F1r. Q2 does not have an ornament to fill space at the bottom of F1v, but a catchword has been added (see Plate 5). The Q2 compositor also changed the indentation of the songs, and introduced pilcrows into the design of two pages, A4v and D4r.[6] In Q1, pilcrows appear as space fillers or decoration only on the title-page, but in Q2 they are inserted on eighteen out of the forty-two pages. The speech headings, abbreviated in both quartos, contain far more stops in Q2, and are more frequently mislined.

[5] Stage directions at ll. 202–3, 499–500 (see Plate 4), 928–9, and 996–9. In Q2, lower-case is sometimes substituted to save space, as in ll. 202 and 243.
[6] For D4r, see Plate 6. Pilcrows are used randomly on C4v, D1v, D4v, and E2r. On occasions the compositor seems to have attempted a visual design, as on C3r, D3r, E1v, and E2v.

It is possible that Q2, although it bears Allde's imprint, was not set in his shop. There are clear differences between the spelling patterns of Q1 and Q2, notwithstanding exigencies of space and availability of type.[7] The spelling 'oo' ('doo' for 'do', and derivates), for example, which is characteristic of Q1 but not of Q2, has been held to be a preferred practice in John Allde's printing house.[8] It may be that Q1 was an in-house edition, and that Q2 was not set by Allde's regular compositor, nor even in the same printing shop. The punctuation of the quartos adds further, albeit slender evidence to support this notion. In Q1, there are many instances where the colon is used inappropriately at the ends of lines. Commenting on the changes made in Allde's shop in the setting of the third quarto of *Jack Juggler*, Ifor Evans and Greg noted that a great deal of punctuation was introduced,

but very mechanically and sometimes incorrectly.... The printer's general notion seems to have been to put a colon at the end of the first line of a couplet (even where it ended a speech) and a full point at the end of the second, with little or no regard for the sense.[9]

This appears to be a similar practice to the one adopted by the compositor in Q1. By contrast, the compositor of Q2 avoided using colons, and produced a smoother, less halting text.[10]

In all, Q1 was set carefully and accurately, although not as neatly as Q2. There were over 1500 changes between the quartos, including alterations in spelling, punctuation, and capitals. Q2 added a number of errors. The evidence suggests that Q3 was set from Q2, and has no independent authority. It agrees overwhelmingly with Q2's changes (see Textual Notes 4, p. 119 below), and follows it in lineation.

The present edition is a 1:1 photofacsimile prepared from photographs of

[7] For example, the following changes from Q1 to Q2 each occur more than ten times (quotations are given in roman): Q2 shortens Q1 'muche' to 'much' (12 times); 'whiche' to 'which' (36); 'iche' to 'ich' (12); 'suche' to 'such' (41); and 'doo' to 'do' (34); Q2 lengthens Q1 'se' to 'see' (32 times) and 'master' to 'maister' (19).

[8] M. St. Clare Byrne, 'Anthony Munday's Spelling as a Literary Clue', *The Library*, 4th series, iv (1924), 9–23 (19–20). The following are examples: 'woords' (l. 26), 'doo' (l. 29), 'woold' (l. 131), 'doon' (l. 169), 'dooings' (l. 241), 'prooue' (l. 410), 'doost' (l. 502), 'woorth' (l. 581), 'woorks' (l. 730), 'dooth' (l. 738), 'sword' (l. 1155), 'looue' (l. 1355), 'abooue' (l. 1357).

[9] *Jack Juggler (Third Edition)*, eds. B. Ifor Evans and W. W. Greg, Malone Society Reprints (Oxford, 1937), p. viii.

[10] The following are typical examples of colons used in Q1: 'ere:' (l. 36), interruption between subject and verb; 'wel:' (l. 82), between verb and direct object; 'passe:' (l. 198), end of speech. In each of these the colon comes after the first line of the couplet. The rationale was probably rhetorical rather than grammatical. Q2 usually substitutes a comma.

the unique copy of Q1 in the Bodleian Library.[11] In the outer margins are through line numbers, counted in tens, from the title on A1r. Catchwords are excluded from the count. Four sets of Textual Notes follow the photofacsimiles. These record lost, doubtful, or illegible readings in Q1, and collations from Q2 and Q3 (see pp. 109–20).[12]

THE AUTHOR

Ulpian Fulwell was born at Wells in Somerset in 1546, the son of Thomas Fulwell who had risen from humble beginnings to become a successful merchant. The fact that Thomas figured in a number of lawsuits against his kinsman John Goodman, from whom he leased land, has made it possible to recover some of the circumstances of his son's life.[13] Ulpian was ordained on 15 September 1566 and became Rector of Naunton in Gloucestershire in 1570 by the gift of the Queen and with Burghley's patronage. His first marriage, to Eleanor Warde in 1572, produced one son. After Eleanor's death in 1577 he married Mary Whorwood, by whom he had six children. His management of the parish attracted unfavourable comment, and he was fined for negligence over teaching, and for the inefficiency of his curate in 1576.

He seems to have sought a public role during the 1570s. In 1575 he published *The Flower of Fame*, a miscellany which praised the Tudor dynasty and its Protestant faith. A friendship developed with Edward Harman who had been Henry VIII's barber and who became a gentleman usher to Edward VI. The book was dedicated to Burghley, perhaps in pursuit of further patronage. In

[11] *Like Will to Like* was first edited, from Q3, in R. Dodsley, *A Select Collection of Old English Plays*, 4th edn., revised edn., W. C. Hazlitt, 15 vols. (London, 1874–6), iii.303–59. J. S. Farmer printed a modernized text of Q1 in *The Dramatic Writings of Ulpian Fulwell* (London, 1906), and reproduced Q3 in the Tudor Facsimile Texts (London, 1909). An old-spelling edition of Q3 was published in *Tudor Interludes*, ed. Peter Happé (Harmondsworth, 1972), and a modernized edition of Q1 in *Four Tudor Interludes*, ed. J. A. B. Somerset (London, 1974).

[12] The '12pt Caslon Black' type used for the Textual Notes formerly belonged to Oxford University Press, Printing Division, when it was given the designation (and named on the cases) '1-nick Pica Old Black'. The type was used in earlier Malone Society editions (most recently the volume for 1984). After the closure of the Printing Division in 1989, the type passed into the keeping of the St Bride Printing Library, London. The Society is most grateful to Mr James Mosley of this Library for permission to use the type, and for making available facilities for typesetting and the preparation of camera-ready copy.

[13] See *DNB*, and Irving Ribner, 'Ulpian Fulwell and his Family', *Notes and Queries*, cxcv (1950), 444–8, and 'Ulpian Fulwell and the Court of High Commission', cxcvi (1951), 268–70; Roberta Buchanan, *'Ars Adulandi, or the Art of Flattery', by Ulpian Fulwell : A Critical Edition with a Biography of the Author* (Salzburg, 1984), gives a family tree, and a list of lawsuits, pp. lxxi–lxxii.

this Fulwell may have been disappointed, for the *Ars Adulandi* (1576) is a satire on flattery and preferment in Church and State. He was censured for this uncomfortably lively work (which was dedicated to Burghley's wife), and on 7 September 1576 he had to make a public recantation in the Court of High Commission in response to the Bishop of Bath and Wells. In spite of his promise of amendment, another edition, somewhat toned down, appeared in 1579. Perhaps this was related to a new search for public success, since he matriculated at St Mary's Hall, Oxford, on 27 March 1579 at the age of 33. He had gained his MA by 1584, but he died before 13 July 1586, when there was a dispute over the Naunton Rectory. The third quarto of *Like Will to Like* appeared in the following year.

Fulwell may have written *Like Will to Like* at around the date of his ordination. He was then in his early twenties, which may account for the mixture of conforming piety and roistering wickedness in the play. At this time, even his mother found his behaviour and that of his brother reprehensible (although she seems to have been a contentious individual herself).

THE PLAY

Like Will to Like has received little detailed critical attention, although it is mentioned in general works on the interlude.[14] It has close similarities with other interludes of the period, yet in many respects it is a distinctive work. Its satirical thrust, and its straightforward doctrinal position link it with Fulwell's two prose works, *The Flower of Fame* and *Ars Adulandi*, but it shows a clear awareness of the theatre. There is no independent evidence of an early production, but the stage directions may indicate that it was written with performance in mind. The reference at ll. 211–12 to playing a 'Gittorn', or some other instrument, suggests at least that Fulwell thought the play might be acted. The text also offers interesting notions about how actors might move around the stage—fighting, riding, dancing, kneeling, card playing, falling over, sitting, snoring, carousing. There is also some attention to properties in the stage directions and dialogue. The direction at ll. 962–4, for example, lists the properties Nichol Newfangle is to bring on stage, and the subsequent action shows him making use of each item.

On its title-page the play was offered as a piece which could be doubled and played by five actors, and it may be that a professional men's company was

[14] See T. W. Craik, *The Tudor Interlude: Stage, Costume, and Acting* (Leicester, 1958), *passim*, and David M. Bevington, *From 'Mankind' to Marlowe : Growth of Structure in the Popular Drama of Tudor England* (Cambridge, Mass., 1962), pp. 155–8.

seen as a prospective purchaser. The comic routines, although conventional, are good examples of what might appeal to professionals. A high standard of musicianship would be required, but this too was probably not beyond what would normally be expected of a touring company. However, the phrase 'in the shroudes' (l. 248) may be a hint that *Like Will to Like* was in fact originally designed (and perhaps produced) as a boys' play at St Paul's.[15]

The plot is very simple and undemanding, yet it turns out to be neat and effective. The Prologue sets the objectives of providing mirth and a good example. This is done in the plotting which brings Lucifer on at the beginning to instruct his godson, Nichol Newfangle the Vice, who is to help to maintain pride and bring like to like, especially among the wicked. The Vice carries out these tasks with successive pairs of characters. Two of the pairs reappear showing how badly things have gone for them. The Vice turns from false promises of land, to destroying the pairs by bringing them to death or beggary. Lucifer reappears and rewards Nichol by taking him off to Hell on his back (l. 1301).[16] By contrast, Virtuous Living describes what he has to offer, and is celebrated by God's Promises, Good Fame, and Honour. The plot is not intrinsically interesting for its intrigue or surprises, and the mode is not naturalistic, but it sustains the action. The chief business is in the character types presented, and in the ways the Vice tricks the characters and shows how they have erred, for the delight and benefit of the audience.

Fulwell gives the Vice a number of opportunities to address the audience, identifying individual members and speaking directly to them, as well as making more general references to 'my masters'.[17] The antics of the other characters are enlivened by dancing, and by four songs which appear to be sung in parts.[18] Two further songs are sung by the virtues. The cast also includes a ruthless judge, Severity, and a comic hangman. Some of the characters—especially Cutpurse, Pickpurse, and Dutch Haunce—are conventional types.

[15] Dr Marie Axton has drawn attention (privately) to the phrase 'in the shroudes' which was associated with the church under St Paul's (*OED* 'shroud' sb.1.4). It is possible that the playhouse of the Paul's Boys was in the cloister from around 1570 (see Reavley Gair, *The Children of Paul's: the Story of a Theatre Company 1553–1608* (Cambridge, 1982), pp. 46–59).

[16] The motif of the ride to Hell on the devil's back occurs in contemporary plays, and much later ones: for example, *Enough is as Good as a Feast*, Greene's *Friar Bacon and Friar Bungay*, and Marston's *Histriomastix*. It was recalled by Jonson in *The Devil is an Ass*, and *The Staple of News*.

[17] See, for example, ll. 63–5, 111–12, 256, 623, 987, and 1177.

[18] On F2v of the surviving copy of Q2 there is music, written in by hand, for a three-part song for counter-tenor, tenor, and bass. This may be a setting for one or both of the songs printed on D3v–D4r and F2r (see A. J. Sabol, 'A Three-Man Song in Fulwell's *Like Will To Like* at the Folger', *Renaissance News*, x (1957), 139–42).

There are references in the play to Cicero, and St Augustine. At a time when the interlude had become a vigorous vehicle for polemic, the play's Protestant doctrine is remarkably restrained. The drunken Latin prayers and exclamations by Haunce are presumably anti-Roman Catholic. That the wicked are punished by the loss of worldly goods is a characteristically Protestant notion: set against this are the prospects offered by Good Fame. The latter is sent by God's Promise, whose presence may have been a reference to the play by John Bale, the leading Protestant dramatist of the previous generation. In the song, God's Promise is associated with the Word (l. 952):

His holy woord is a perfect ground,

and significantly he extends this into Protestant politics by praising virtuous rulers. Virtuous Living is set in a chair, and is offered a crown and a sword. Although the prayer for Queen, Council, Lords Temporal and Spiritual, and the Commons is conventional, it is thus part of Protestant orthodoxy.

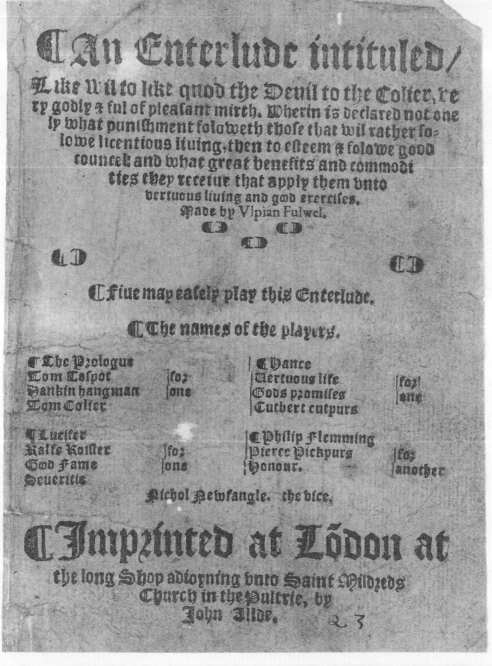

¶An Enterlude intituled/
Like Wil to like quod the Deuil to the Colier, re
ry godly & ful of pleasant mirth. Wherin is declared not one
ly what punishment foloweth those that wil rather folowe licentious liuing, then to esteem & folowe good
councell and what great benefits and commodi
ties they receiue that apply them vnto
vertuous liuing and god exercises.
Made by Vlpian Fulwel.

¶Fiue may easely play this Enterlude.

¶The names of the players.

¶The Prologus			¶Hance		
Tom Tospot	for		Vertuous life	for	
Hankin hangman	one		Gods promises	one	
Tom Colier			Cutbert cutpurs		
¶Lucifer			¶Philip Flemming		
Ralfe Roister	for		Pierce Pickpurs	for	
God Fame	one		Honour.	another	
Seueritie					

Nichol Newfangle. the vice,

¶Imprinted at Lódon at
the long Shop adioyning vnto Saint Mildreds
Church in the Pultrie, by
John Allde.

PLATE 3: TITLE-PAGE OF THE SECOND QUARTO, Q2, OF *LIKE WILL TO LIKE*
(SIG. A1r = LINES 1 TO 23 IN Q1)

¶ He singeth the first two lines and speaketh the rest
as stammeringly as may be.

¶ Quas in hart and quas again and quas about the house a:
And tosse the black bole to and fro e J brinks them all carous a,
Be go go gogs nowns ch ch cha drunk so so much to day: Hau
That be be masse ch chã a moste drunk ich da da dare say,
Chud spe spe spend a goo goo good grote:
Tha that ich cub vi vind my ca ca captain to to tom tospot
¶ Sit down good Hauce lest þ lie on the ground, | he setteth
He knoweth not tom tospot J dare ieobard rr.li. | vi in þ chair
¶ He wil knowe me by and by J holde you a crown   C.
How doost thou seruant Hauncer how cumes this to passe:
Ma ma master to to tom ch ch chã glad vp vp mas. | he driketh Ha
Ca ca carous to to to thee goo goo good Tom,
¶ Holde vp Haunce J wil pledge thee anon.   C.
¶ Wel there is no remedy but J must be gone.   R.
¶ Ta ta tary good below, a wo wo word or twain: Ha
It tho tho thou thy selt do do voo not come a gain.

PLATE 4: PORTION OF SIG. C1r OF Q2 (=LINES 491 TO 508 IN Q1)

ne. ¶ Oh Lord preserue the commons of this Realme also,
Poure vpon them thy heauenly grace:
To aduaunce vertue and vice to ouerthrowe,
That at last in Heauen with thee they may haue place.

Amen.

¶   ¶ Finis. Ɋ Vlpian Fulwel.

A Song

PLATE 5: PORTION OF SIG. F1v OF Q2 (=LINES 1330 TO 1335 IN Q1)

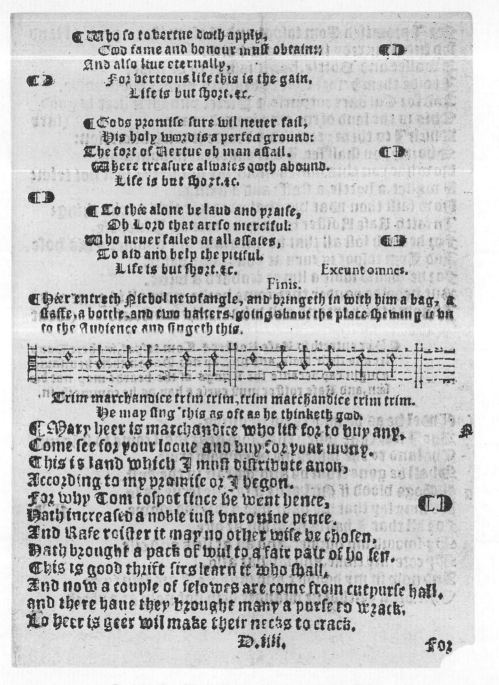

Who so to vertue doth apply,
God fame and honour must obtain:
And also liue eternally,
For verteous life this is the gain.
Life is but short. &c.

Gods promise sure wil neuer fail,
His holy word is a perfect ground:
The fort of Vertue oh man assail,
Where treasure alwaies qwoth abound.
Life is but short. &c.

To thee alone be laud and praise,
Oh Lord that art so merciful:
Who neuer failed at all assaies,
To aid and help the pitiful.
Life is but short. &c.

Finis.   Exeunt omnes.

Theer entreth Nichol newfangle, and bringeth in with him a bag, a staffe, a bottle, and two halters, going about the place shewing it vnto the Audience and singeth this.

Trim marchandice trim trim, trim marchandice trim trim.
He may sing this as oft as he thinketh good.

Mary heer is marchandice who list for to buy any,
Come see for your looue and buy for your mony.
This is land which I must distribute anon,
According to my promise or I begon.
For why Tom tospot since he went hence,
Hath increased a noble iust vnto nine pence.
And Rafe roister it may no other wise be chosen,
Hath brought a pack of wul to a fair pair of ho sen.
This is good thrift sirs learn it who shall,
And now a couple of felowes are come from cutpurse hall,
and there haue they brought many a purse to wrack,
Lo heer is geer wil make their necks to crack.

D.iiii.   For

PLATE 6: SIG. D4r OF Q2 (= LINES 946 TO 978 IN Q1)

The 1568 Quarto Edition
of
an Interlude entitled

Like Will to Like

¶ An Enterlude Intituled,

Like wil to like quod the Deuel to the Colier, vn-
godly and ful of plesant mirth. Wherin is declared not onely what punishement followeth those that wil rather followe licentious liuing, then to esteem & followe good
councel: and what great benefits and commodi
ties they receiue that apply them vnto
vertuous liuing and god exercises.
Made by Ulpian Fulwel.

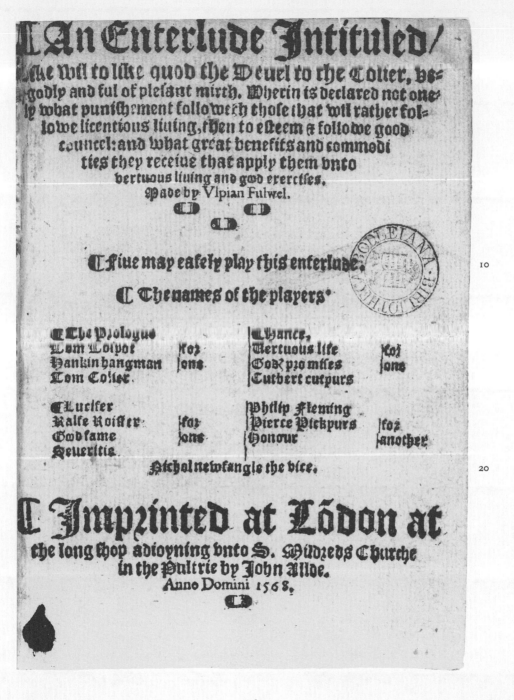

¶ fiue may easely play this enterlude.

¶ The names of the players.

¶ The Prologue		¶ Hance,	
Tom Toipot	for	Uertuous life	for
Hankin hangman	ons.	God promises	ons
Tom Collier.		Cuthbert cutpurs	
¶ Lucifer		Philip Fleming	
Ralfe Roister	for	Pierce Pickpurs	for
God fame	ons	Honour	another
Seueritie.			

Nichol newfangle the vice.

¶ Imprinted at Lōdon at

the long shop adioyning vnto S. Mildreds Churche
in the Pultrie by John Allde.
Anno Domini 1568.

Cicero in his book de amicitia these woozds dooth expzesse,
Saying nothing is moze desirous then like is vnto like
Whose woozds are moste true & of a certaintie doutles
foz the vertuous doo not the vertuous company mislike.
But the vicious doo the vertuous company eschue: 30
And like wil vnto like this is moste true.
It is not my meaning your eares foz to wery,
With harkening what is theffect of our matter:
But our pzetence is to mooue you to be mery
Merely to speak meaning no man to flatter.
The name of this matter as I said while ere:
Is like wil to like quoth the Deuel to the Colier.
Sith pithy pzouerbs in our Englische tung dooth abound   40
Our authour thought good suche a one foz to chuse:
As may shew good exsample and mirth may eke be found,
But no lasciuious toyes he purposeth foz to vse,
Heer in as it were in a glasse se you may :
The aduauncement of vertuo of vice the decay.
To what ruin ruffians and roisters are bzought,
You may heer se of them the finall end
Begging is the best though that end be nought,
But hanging is wurse if they doo not amend.
The vertuous life is bzought to honour and dignitie:
And at the last to euerlasting eternitie.
And becaule diuers men of diuers mindes be,   50
Some doo matters of mirth and pastime require:
Other some are delighted with matters of grauitie,
To please all men is our authours cheef desire.
Wherfoze mirth with measure to sadnes is annexed:
Desiring that none heer at our matter wilbe perplexed.
Thus as I said I wil be shozt and bzeef,
Because from this dump you shall releaued be :

A.ii,   And

... with the Colias the thee that kepe...

Shall soon make you mery as shortly you shall se,
And sith mirth for sadnes is a sauce moste sweet,
Take mirth then with measure that best sauceth it.

¶Finis.

¶ Hær entreth Nichol Newfangle the vice laughing, & hath
knaue of clubs in his hand whiche assone as he speaketh: he of
fereth vnto one of the men or boyes standing by.

Ha, ha, ha, ha, now like vnto like it wilbe none other,
Stoup gentle knaue and take vp your brother.
Why is it so: and is it euen so in deede:
Why then may I say God send vs good speed.
And is euery one heer so greatly vnkinde,
That I am no soner out of sight but quite out of minde:
Mary this wil make a man euen weep for wo,
That on suche a sudain no man wil me knowe.
Sith men be so daungerous now at this day:
Yet are women kinde wormes I dare wel say.
How say you woman: you that stand in the angle,
Were you neuer acquainted with Nichol newfangle:
Then I se Nichol newfangle is quite forgot,
Yet you wil knowe me anone I dare ieobard a grote.
Nichol newfangle is my name, doo you not me knowe:
My whole education to you I shall showe.
For first before I was borne I remember very wel:
That my gransire and I made a iourney into hel.
Where I was bound prentice before my natiuitie,
To Lucifer him self suche was my agilitie.
All kinde of sciences he taught vnto me:
That vnto the maintainance of pride might best agree.
I learnd to make gownes with long sleeues and winges:
I learnd to make ruffes like calues chitterlings:
Caps, hats, cotes with all kinde of apparails,

And

68

Shoos, boots, buskins, with many pretie toyes:
All kinde of garments for men, women and boyes.
Knowe you be now? I thought that at the last:
All acquaintance from Nichol newfangle is not past.
Nichol newfangle was and is, and euer shallbe:
And there are but few that are not acquainted with me.
For so soon as my prentishod was once come out:
I went by and by the whole world about.

       Heer the Deuil entreth in but hee speaketh
               not yet. 100

¶ Sancte benedicite, whom haue we heer?
Tom tumbler or els some dauncing bear?
Body of me it were best go no near :
For ought that I see it is my godfather Lucifer.
Whose prentice I haue been this many a day: (say.
But no mo woords but mum, you shall hear what he wil

     ¶ This name Lucifer must bo written on his back and in
         his brest.

¶ Ho myne owne boy I am glad that thou art heer: 110
¶ He speaketh to you sir I pray you come neer : |pointig to one
¶ Nay þ art euen he of whom I am wel apaid: |standing by.
¶ Then speak a loof of for to come nie I am afrayd.
¶ Why so nie boy? as though thou didst neuer se me?
¶ Yes godfather but I am afraid it is now as oft times it is
For if my dame and þ hast bee tubling by yeares   (to thee
As often times you doo like a couple of great beares.
Thou carest not whom thou killest in thy raging minde:
Doost thou not remember since þ didst bruse me behinde?
This hole in thy furp didst thou disclose,
That now in a tent be put in so big as thy nose.
This was when my dame called thee bottle nosed knaue,
           J.iii.   But

120

But I am not to tary the mater to my ground

¶ Oh my good boy be not afraid,
For no suche thing hath happened as thou hast said:
But come to me my boy and blesse thee I wil,
And see that my precepts thou doo fulfil,

¶ Wel godfather if you wil say ought to me in this cace,
Speak for in faith I mean not to kneel to that il face
If our Lady of Walsingham had no fairer nose and visage,
By the masse they were fooles p woold go to her on pilgre-
                                                    (mage

¶ Wel boy it shall not greatly fail,
Whether thou stand or whether thou kneel:
Thou knowest what sciences I haue thee taught,
Whiche are able to bring the world to naught.
For thou knowest p through pride from heuen I was cast,
Euen vnto hel wherfore se thou make haste
Suche pride through new factions in mens harts to sowe,
That those that vse it may haue the like ouerthrowe.
From vertue procure men to set their mindes aside,
And wholy imploy it to all sin and pride
Let thy new fangled sations bear suche a sway,
That a raskall be so proud as he that best may.

¶ Tushe, tushe, that is all ready brought to passe,
For a very skipiack is prouder I swear by the masse,
And seeketh to go more gayer and more braue,
Then dooth a Lord though him self be a knaue.

¶ I can thee thank that so wel thou hast playd thy part,
Suche as doo so, shall soon feel the smart:
Sith thou hast thus doon there remaineth behinde,
That thou in another thing shew thy right kinde.

¶ Then good godfather let me heer thy minde,

¶ Thou knowest I am bothe proud and arrogant,
And with the proud I wil euer be conuersant,
I cannot abide to see men that are vitious,

                                        Accompany

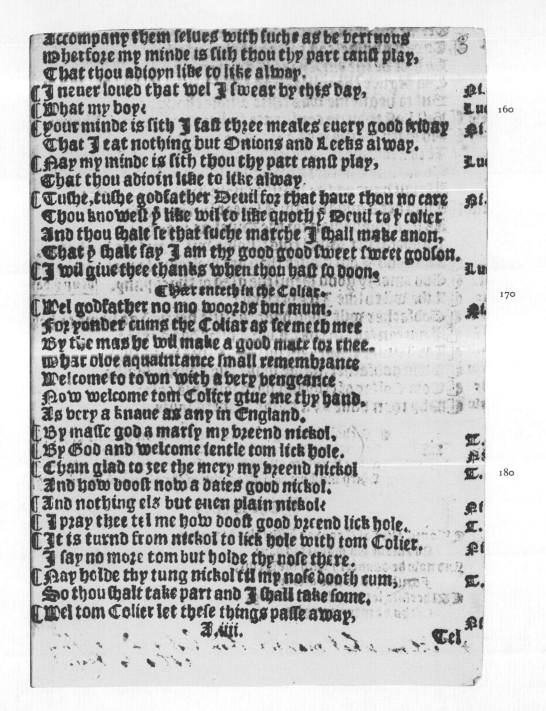

accompany them selues with suche as be vertuous
wherfore my minde is sith thou thy part canst play,
That thou adioyn like to like alway.

[¶I neuer loued that wel I swear by this day, — Ni.

[¶What my boye — Luc. 160

[¶your minde is sith I fast three meales euery good friday — Ni.
That I eat nothing but Onions and Leeks alway.

[¶Nay my minde is sith thou thy part canst play, — Luc
That thou adioin like to like alway.

[¶Tushe, tushe godfather Deuil for that haue thou no care — Ni.
Thou knowest ð like wil to like quoth ð Deuil to ð colier
And thou shalt se that suche matche I shall make anon,
That ð shalt say I am thy good good sweet sweet godson.

[¶I wil giue thee thanks when thou hast so doon — Luc

Ther enteth in the Coliar. 170

[¶Wel godfather no mo woordes but mum, — Ni.
For yonder cums the Coliar as seemeth mee
By the mas he wil make a good mate for thee.
what olde aquaintance small remembrance
Welcome to town with a very vengeance
Now welcome tom Colier giue me thy hand,
As very a knaue as any in England.

[¶By masse god a marsy my freend nickol, — T. Ni.

[¶By God and welcome ientle tom lick hole.

[¶Cham glad to zee the mery my freend nickol — T. 180
And how doost now a daies good nickol.

[¶And nothing els but euen plain nickole — Ni.

[¶I pray thee tel me how doost good freend lick hole. — T.

[¶It is turnd from nickol to lick hole with tom Colier. — Ni.
I say no more tom but holde thy nose there.

[¶Nay holde thy tung nickol til my nose dooth cum, — T.
So thou shalt take part and I shall take some.

[¶Wel tom Colier let these things passe away, — Ni.

I.iiii.

Tel.

✠ Tel me what market thou hast made of thy coles to day.

¶ To euery bushel cha solde but thzee peck:
   Lo heer be the empty sacks on my neck.
   Cha begilde the whozesons that of me ha bought,
   But to begile me was their whole thought.

¶ But hast thou no conscience in begiling thy neighbours

¶ No mary so iche may gaines boz my labour,
   It is a common trade now adaies this is plain:
   To cut one anothers thzote foz luker and gain.
   I small baut as the wozld is now brought to passe:

¶ Thou art a good fellow I swear by the masse.
   As fit a companion foz the Diuel as may be:
   Lo godfather Diuel this fellowe wil I matche with thee.

¶ And good Tom Colier thou art welcome to me: *Hee taketh*

¶ God amarzy good Deuil cha glad of thy cõpany.   *hi by y hã*

¶ Like wil to like I see very wel:

¶ Godfather wilt thou daūce a little befoze y go home to hel

¶ I am content so that Tom Colier doo agree:

¶ I wil neuer refuse (Deuil) to daunce with thee.

¶ Then godfather, name what the daunce shalbe,

¶ Tom Collar of croydon hath solde his cole:

¶ Why then haue at it by my fathers soule.

¶ Nichol newfangle must haue a Gittozn oz some other in
strument (if it may bee) but if hee haue not they must daūce
about the place all thzee, and sing this song that followeth
which must bee don also althoug they haue an instrumēt.

¶ The Song.

¶ Tom Colier of Croydon hath solde his coles,
   And made his market to day:
And now he daunceth with the Deuil,
   Foz like wil to like alway.
¶ Wherfoze let vs reioyce and sing,
   Let vs be mery and glad:

✠ Tell me whet markit thow hast mady of thy
coles to-dey.

72

Sing that the Colier and the Deuil,
   This matche and daunce hath made.
❡ Now of this daunce we make an end,
   With mirth and eke with ioy:
The Colier and the Deuil wilbe,
   Muche like to like alway.   ❡ Finis.

❡ A ha, mary this is trim singing,
  I had not thought the Deuil to be so cunning.
  And by the masse Tom Colier as good as he: 230
  I see that like with like wil euer agree.
❡ Farwel master Deuil for iche must be gone. Exit.
❡ Why then farwel my gentle freend Tom.
❡ Farwel Tom Colier a knaue be thy comfort,
  How saist thou godfather is not this trim sport:
❡ Thou art myne owne boy my blessing thou shalt haue:
❡ By my trouth godfather that blessing I doo not craue.
  But if you go your way I wil doo my diligence:
  As wel in your absence as in your presence.
❡ But thou shalt salute me or I go doutles: 240
  That in thy dooings thou maist haue the better succes.
  Wherfore kneel down and say after me:
❡ When ʒ deuil wil haue it so it must needs so be. He kneleth
  What shal I say bottle nosed godfather cast ʒ tel. down.
❡ Ill hail oh noble prince of hel,
❡ All my dames cowes tail fel down in the wel.
❡ I wil exalt thee aboue the clouds :
❡ I wil salte thee and hang thee in the shroudes.
❡ Thou art the inhaunser of my renown :
❡ Thou art haunce the hangman of Callice town.   250
❡ To thee be honour alone:
❡ To thee shall come our hobling Ione.
❡ Amen.
❡ Amen.
❡ Now farwel my boy farwel hartely.
                    B.i.   Is

Is there neuer a knaue heer wil keep the deuil companye
Far wel godfather for thou must go alone
I pray thee come hither again anon.   Exit Lucifer.
Mary heer was a benediction of the deuils good grace,
260   Body of me I was so afraid I was like to be stenche ý place
My buttocks made buttous of the new fation,
While the whorson Deuil was making his salutation.
But by masse I am so glad as euer was madge mare,
That the whorson Deuil is ioyned with the knaue Collar
As fit a matche as euer could be pickt out,
What saist thou to it Jone with the long snout:

     Tom Tospot commeth in with a fether in his hat.
But who comes yonder puffing as whot as a black pudding
I holde xx.li. it is a ruffin if a Goose go a gooding.
270   Gogs hart and his guts is not this to bad:
Blood, wounds and nailes, it wil make a man mad.
I warrant you heer is a lustie one very braue,
I think anon he wil swear him self a knaue.
Many a mile haue I ridden, & many a mile haue I gone:
Yet can I not kinde for me a fit companion,
Many therbe whiche my company would frequent:
If to doo as they doo I would be content.
They would haue mee leaue of my pride and my swearing
My new fangled fations and leaue of this wearing.
280   But rather then I suche companions wil haue.
I wil se a thousand of them laid in their graue.
Similis similem sibi quærit, suche a one doo I seek,
As vnto my self in euery condition is like.
Sir you are welcome ye seem to be an honest man,
And I wil help you in this matter asmuche as I can
If you wil tary heer a while I tel you in good sooth,
I wil finde one as fit for you as a pudding for a friers
I thank you my freend for your gentle offer to me. (mouth
                                              I

I pray you tel me what your name may be.

¶We think by your apparel you haue had me in regard. 290

I pray you of Nichol newfangle haue you neuer hearde

¶Nichol new fangle? why we are of olde acquaintance,

¶By my trothe your name is quite out of my remembrance.

¶At your first comming into England wel I wot,

You were very wel acquainted with Tom tospot.

¶Tom tospot? Sancti amen, how you were out of my minde

You know whē you brought into ēglād this new fāgled kinde

That tospots & ruffians with you were first acquainted.

¶It is euen so Tom tospot as thou hast said.

¶It is an olde saying that mountains & hilles neuer meet, 300

But I se that men shall meet though they doo not seek

And I promise you more ioy in my hart I haue found,

Then if I had gayned an hundreth pound.

¶And I am as glad as one had giuen me a grote,

That I haue met now with thee Tom tospot

And seeing that thou wouldst a mate so fain haue,

I wil ioyn thee with one that shalbe as very a knaue,

As thou art thy self thou maist beleeue me:

Thou shalt se anone what I wil doo for thee.

For you seek for as very a knaue as you your self are, 310

For like wil to like quoth the Deuil to the Coliar.

¶In deed nichol newfangle ye say ye veritie, | Her entreth
                                              | Rafe Roister

For like wil to like it wil none other wise be.

¶Beholde tom tospot euen in pudding time,

Yonder commeth Rafe Roister an olde freend of mine

By the masse for thee he is so fit a mate,

As Tom and Tib for Bit and Kate,

Now welcome my freend Rafe Roister by the masse.

¶And I am glad to see thee heer in this place.

¶Bid him welcome, hark he can play a knaues part. 320

¶My freend you are welcome with all my hart,

B.ii.   ¶God

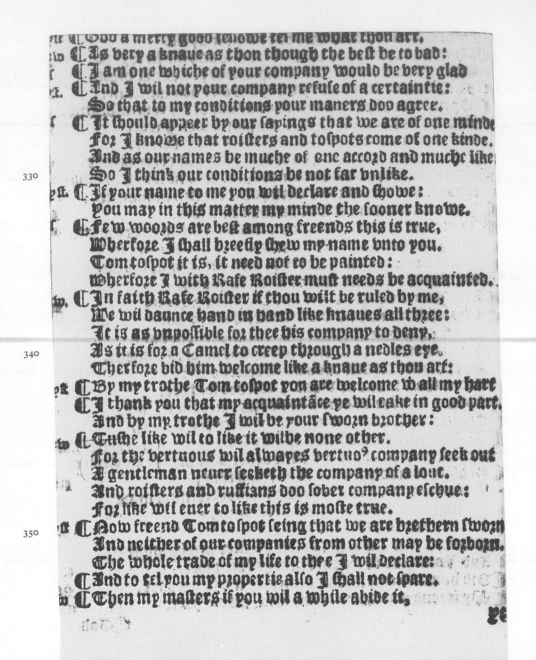

¶ God a mercy good fellowe tel me what thou art.

¶ As very a knaue as thou though the best be to bad:

¶ I am one whiche of your company would be very glad

¶ And I wil not your company refuse of a certaintie:
   So that to my conditions your maners doo agree.

¶ It should appeer by our sayings that we are of one minde
   For I knowe that roisters and tospots come of one kinde.
   And as our names be muche of one accord and muche like

330
   So I think our conditions be not far vnlike.

¶ If your name to me you wil declare and showe:
   You may in this matter my minde the sooner knowe.

¶ Few woords are best among freends this is true,
   Wherfore I shall breefly shew my name vnto you.
   Tom tospot it is, it need not to be painted:
   wherfore I with Rafe Roister must needs be acquainted.

¶ In faith Rafe Roister if thou wilt be ruled by me,
   We wil daunce hand in hand like knaues all three:
   It is as vnpossible for thee his company to deny,

340
   As it is for a Camel to creep through a nedles eye.
   Therfore bid him welcome like a knaue as thou art:

¶ By my trothe Tom tospot you are welcome vv all my hart

¶ I thank you that my acquaintāce ye wil take in good part.
   And by my trothe I wil be your sworn brother:

¶ Tushe like wil to like it wilbe none other.
   For the vertuous wil alwayes vertuo⁹ company seek out
   A gentleman neuer seeketh the company of a lout.
   And roisters and ruffians doo sober company eschue:
   For like wil euer to like this is moste true.

350
¶ Now freend Tom tospot seing that we are brethern sworn
   And neither of our companies from other may be forborn.
   The whole trade of my life to thee I wil declare:

¶ And to tel you my propertie also I shall not spare.

¶ Then my masters if you wil a while abide it,

ye mall se two suche knaues so liuely described,
That if hel should be raked euen by and by indeed :
Suche another couple cãnot bo found I swear by my creed,
Go to sirs say on your whole mindes
And I shall paint you out in your right kindes,
First Tom tospot plead thou thy cause and thy name :
And I wil sit in this chair and giue sentence on the same. 360
I wil play the iudge and in this matter giue iudgement :
How say you my masters are you not so content:
¶ By my trothe for my part therto I doo agree: K.
¶ I wear to blame if any fault should be in me.   T.
¶ Then that I be in office neither of you doo grudge :   N
¶ No in deed.   Bi
¶ where learnd you to stand capt before a iudge.   N
  you souterly knaues shewe you all your maners at once:
¶ Why Nichol all we are content,   K. 370
¶ And am I plain Nichol: and yet it is in my arbitrement,   N
  to iudge whiche of you two is the veryer knaue.
I am master Nichol newfangle bothe gay and braue.
For seeing you make me your iudge I trowe :
I shal teache you bothe your litripup to knowe.   [He fighteth]
¶ Stay your self sir I pray you hartely :   T
¶ I pray you be content and we wilbe more manerly   K N
¶ Nay I cannot put vp suche an iniury.   N
For seing I am in office I wil be known therfore: [He fighteth
send your heds sirs for I wil to it once more.   again. 380
¶ I pray you be content good gentle master Nichol :   K T N
¶ I neuer saw the like by gogs soule,   N
¶ wel my masters because you doo intend,   N
To learn good maners and your conditions to amend.
I wil haue but one fit more & so make an end.   [He fighteth
¶ I pray you sir let vs no more contend,   again.]   K
¶ Mary this hath brethed me very wel: N
                        B.iii,   Now

Now let me hear now your tales ye can tel.
And I master Judge wil so bring to passe

That I wil iudge who shalbe knaue of clubs at Christma
☞ Gogs wounds I am like Phalaris that made a Bul of brasse
☞ Thou art like a false knaue now, and euermore was,
☞ Nay I am like Phalaris that made a bul of brasse,
As a cruel torment for suche as did offend
And he him self first there in put was,
Euen so are we brought now to this end.
In ordayning him a iudge, who wilbe honoured as a God
So for our owne tailes we haue made a rod.
☞ And I am serued as Haman that preparde,
☞ How was he serued I pray thee doo me tel,
☞ Who I speak of thou knowest not wel,
☞ Thou art serued as Hatry hangman captain of the black
garde
☞ Nay I am serued as Haman that prepared,
A high pair of Gallowes for Mardocheus the Iew:
And was the first him self that there on was hanged,
So I feel the smart of myne owne rod this is true.
But heerafter I wil learn to be wise,
And ere I leap once I wil look twice.
☞ Wel Tom tospot first let me heer thee,
How canst thou prooue thy self a verier knaue then he
☞ You knowe that tom tospot men doo me call,
☞ A knaue thou hast alwayes been and euermore shall.
☞ My conditions I am sure ye knowe as wel as I
☞ A knaue thou was born and so thou shalt die.
☞ But that you are a iudge I would say vnto you,
Knaues are christen men els you were a Iew.
☞ He calles me knaue by craft, doo you not see
Sira I wil remember it when you think not on me.
Wel say what thou canst for thyne owne behoof,
If thou proouest thy self the veryer knaue by good proof.
Thou

Thou must be the elder brother and haue the patrimony,
And when he hath said then doo thou reply
Euen Thomas a wateringes or Tiburn hil,
To the falsest theef of you bothe by my fathers wil,
I pray you sir what is that patrimony? R.R.
I pray you leaue your curtesy & I wil tel you by an by, Ni.?
If he be the more knaue, the patrimony he must haue
But p shalt haue it if thou proue thy self the verier knaue,
A peece of ground it is that of beggers manner doo holde,
And who so deserues it shall haue it ye may be bolde
Caild saint Thomas a watrings or els Tiburn hil, 430
Giuen and so bequeathed to the falshest knaue by wil.
Then I trowe I am he that this patrimony shall posses L.L
for I Tom tospot doo vse this trade doutles:
from morning til night I sit tossing the black bole,
Then come I home and pray for my fathers soule.
Saying my prayers with woundes, blood, guts and hart,
Swearing and staring thus play I my part.
If any poor man haue in a whole week earnd one grote, 440
He shall spend it in one houre in tossing the pot.
I vse to call seruants and poor men to my company:
And make them spend all they haue vnthriftely.
So that my company they think to be so good
That in short space their here growes through their hood.
But wil no gossips keep thee company now an than, Ni.
Tushe I am acquainted with many a woman, L.L
That with me wil sit in euery house and place
But then their husbands had need fend their face,
for when they come home they wil not be a ferd, 450
To shake the goodman, and sometime shaue his beard,
And as for flemishe seruants I haue suche a train,
That wil quasse and carous and therin spend their gain.
from week to week I haue all this company,

                    B.iiii.   Wherfore

79

Wherfore I am worthy to haue the patrimony.

¶Thus thou maist be called a knaue in grain,
And where knaues are scant thou shalt go for twain.
But now Rafe roister let me hear what thou canst say:

¶You knowe that Rafe roister I am called alway,
And my conditions in knauery so far dooth surmount:

460 That to haue this patrimony I make myne account.
For I entice yung gentlemen all vertue to eschue :
And to giue them selues to riotousnes this is true.
Seruing men also by me are so seduced:
That all in brauery their mindes are confused.
Then if they haue not them selues to maintain :
To pick and to steal they must be fain.
And I may say to you I haue suche a train:
That sometime I pitche a feeld on Salisbury plain,
And muche more if need were I could say verely:

470 Wherfore I am worthy to haue the patrimony.
Ho that shall iudge this matter had need haue more wit the[n]
But seeing you haue referred it vnto my arbitrement
In faith I wil giue suche equall iudgement :
That bothe of you shalbe wel pleased and content,

¶May I haue not doon, for I can say muche more
¶Wel I wil not haue you contend any more.
But this ferm whiche to beggers maner dooth apertain:
I wil equally deuide between you twain.
Are you not content that so it shall be?

480 ¶As it pleaseth you so shall we agree.
¶Then se that anon ye come bothe vnto me.
¶Sir for my part I thank you hartely,
I promised of late to come vnto a company.
Whiche at Hob filchers for me doo remain:
God be with you and anon I wil come again,
¶Farwel brother Rafe I wil come to you anon:

Com

Come again for you shall not so sudenly begon,
Se ye not who cus yonder an olde freed of yours?
One that is ready to quasse at all houres.

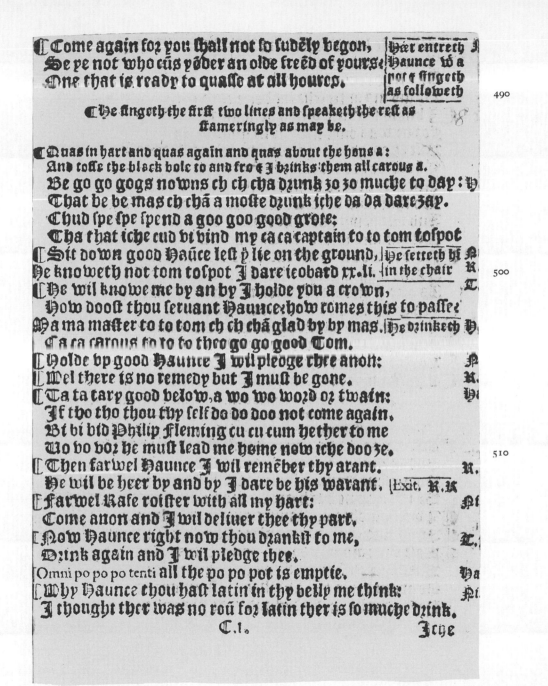

¶ Haer entreth Haunce with a pot & singeth as followeth

The singeth the first two lines and speaketh the rest as stameringly as may be.

Quas in hart and quas again and quas about the hous a:
And tosse the black bole to and fro & I brinks them all carous a.
Be go go gogs nowns ch ch cha drunk zo zo muche to day: y
That be be mas ch cha a moste drunk iche da da darezay.
Chud spe spe spend a goo goo good grote:
Tha that iche cud vi bind my ca ca captain to to tom tospot

Sit down good Haunce lest y lie on the ground,
He knoweth not tom tospot I dare ieobard xx. li.

He setteth him in the chair

He wil knowe me by an by I holde you a crown,
How doost thou seruant Haunce:how comes this to passe?
Ma ma master to to tom ch ch cha glad by by mas.
Ca ca carous to to to thro go go good Tom.

He drinketh

Holde vp good Haunce I wil pledge thee anon:
Wel there is no remedy but I must be gone.
Ta ta tary good below, a wo wo word or twain:
If tho tho thou thy self do do doo not come again,
Bi bi bid Philip Fleming cu cu cum hether to me
Uo vo vor he must lead me home now iche doo ze.
Then farwel Haunce I wil remeber thy arant.
He wil be heer vp and by I dare be his warant.

Exit. R.R

Farwel Rafe roister with all my hart:
Come anon and I wil deliuer thee thy part.
Now Haunce right now thou drankst to me,
Drink again and I wil pledge thee.
Omni po po po tenti all the po po pot is emptie.
Why Haunce thou hast latin in thy belly me think:
I thought ther was no rou for latin ther is so muche drink.

C.i.   Iche

81

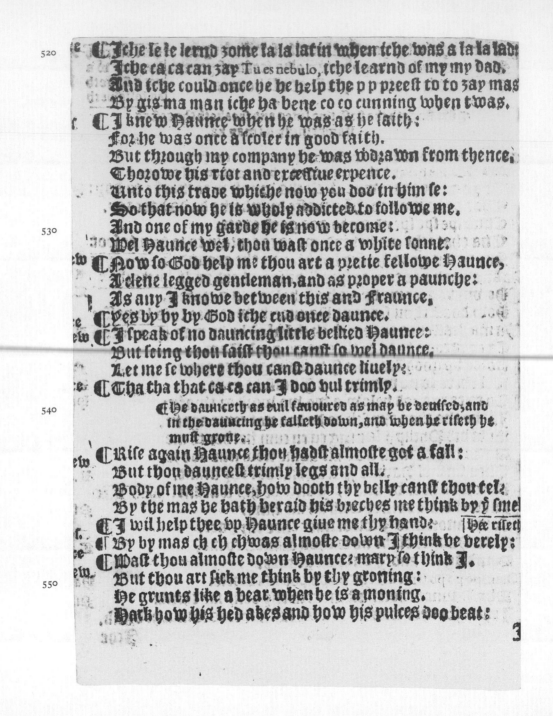

Iche le le lernd some la la latin when iche was a la la lad:
Iche ca ca can say Tu es nebulo, iche learnd of my my dad,
And iche could once he he help the p p preest to to say mas
By gis ma man iche ha bene co co cunning when twas.

¶I knew Haunce when he was as he saith:
For he was once a scoler in good faith.
But through my company he was wdrawn from thence,
Thorowe his riot and excessiue expence.
Unto this trade whiche now you dou in him se:
So that now he is wholy addicted to followe me.
And one of my garde he is now become:
Wel Haunce wel, thou wast once a white sonne.

¶Now so God help me thou art a prettie fellowe Haunce,
A clene legged gentleman, and as proper a paunche:
As any I knowe between this and Fraunce,
¶Yes by by by God iche cud once daunce.

¶I speak of no dauncing little bellied Haunce:
But seing thou saist thou canst so wel daunce,
Let me se where thou canst daunce liuely:
¶Tha tha that ca ca can I doo hul trimly.

　　¶He daunceth as euil fauoured as may be deuised, and
　　in the dauncing he falleth down, and when he riseth he
　　must grone.

¶Rise again Haunce thou hadst almoste got a fall:
But thou dauncest trimly legs and all.
Body of me Haunce, how dooth thy belly canst thou tel:
By the mas he hath beraid his breches me think by ye smel
¶I wil help thee vp Haunce giue me thy hand:　　[He riseth
¶By by mas ch ch chwas almoste down I think be verely:
¶Wast thou almoste down Haunce: mary so think I.
But thou art sick me think by thy groning:
He grunts like a bear when he is a moning.
Hark how his hed akes and how his pulces doo beat:

3

I ruinn he wil be hangd his belly is so great.

❧Go go god amerey good Tom with all my hart:

❧If thou canst not leap Haunce, let me se thee drink a quart
And get thee out abrode into the air:

❧Tushe he had more need to sleep in this chair.
Sit down Haunce and thou shalt se anon:
Philip flemming wil come to fetche thee home.

❧Haunce sitteth in the chair, and snorteth as though
he were fast a sleep.

❧I pray thee Tom tospot is this one of thy men?

❧He is a companion of mine now and then.

❧By the faith of my body, suche Carpenter suche chips,
And as the wise man said, suche letice suche lips.
For like master like man, like tutor, like scholler
And like wil to like quoth the Deuil to the Coliar.

❧It is no remedy for it must needs so be:
Like wil to like you may beleeue me.

❧Philip Flemming entreth with a pot in his hand.

❧Lo where Philip Fleming commeth euen in pudding time:

❧He bringeth in his hand eyther good ale or els good wine.

❧Philip Flemming singeth these foure lines
following.

❧Troll the bole and drink to mee, and trole the bole again,
And put a brown taste in the pot, for Philip Flemmings brain,
And I shall tosse it to and fro, euen round about the hous a:
God hostice now let it be so, I drink them all carous a.

❧Mary heer is a pot of noppy good ale:
As cleer as Christall pure and stale.

Now a crab in the fire were wooth a good grote:
That I might quasse with my captain Tom tospot.
What? I can no sooner wishe, but by and by I haue
God saue myne eye sight me think I see a knaue.
C.ii.

What

What captain how goeth the world with you?

¶Why now I see the olde prouerb to be true :
  Like wil to like bothe with Christian, Turk and Iew.
¶Mary Philip euen as I was wunt to doo:
¶Rafe roister tolde me that I should finde Haunce heer,
  where is he that he dooth not appeer?
¶I holde xx.li. the knaue is blinde.
  Turn about Philip Fleming and look behinde.
  Hast thou drunk so muche that thy eyes be out?
  Lo how he snoreth like a lazy lout.
  Go to him for he sleepeth sound :
  Two suche paunches in all England can scant be found.
¶Why Haunce art thou in thy prayers so deuoutly?
  I wake man and we two wil quaffe together stoutly.
¶Domine dominus noster:
  Me think I cha spide three knaues on a cluster,
¶Stay a while for he saith his Pater noster.
¶Sanctum benedicitum what haue I dreamed?
  By gogs nowns chad thought iche had been in my bed.
  Cha dreamed zuche a dream as ý wilt maruel to heer,
  Me thought iche was drowned in a barel of beer.
  And by and by the barel was turned to a ship,
  Whiche me thought the winde made liuely to skip.
  And iche did sail therin from Flaunders to Fraunce :
  At last iche was brought hether among a sort of knaues by
¶Lo Haunce heer is Philip Fleming come now,   (chaunce.
  We wil go drink together now, how saist thou?
¶I pray thee good Uilip now lead me away :
¶Giue me thy hand and I wil thee stay.
¶How say you master Nichol wil you keep vs companye?
¶Go before master lickhole and I wil come by and by.
  Mates matched together depart you three,
  I wil come after you may beleeue me.
                                They

¶ Ha ha ha ha ha ha ha ha,

620

Now three knaues are gone, and I am left alone,

My self heer to solace:

Wel done gentle Ione, why begin you to mone,

Though they be gone I am in place.

And now wil I daunce, now wil I praunce,

For why I haue none other woozk:

Snip snap butter is no bone meat,

Knaues fleshe is no pozke.

Hey tisty tosty an owle is a bird,

Jack a napes hath an olde face:

630

You may beleeue me at one bare woozd,

How like you this mery cace.

A peece of ground they think they haue found,

I wil tel you what it is:

For I them tolde ot beggers maner it did holde,

A staffe and a wallet iwis,

Whiche in shozt space, euen in this place,

Of me they shall receiue:

For when that their drift, hath spent all their thzift,

Their mindes I shall deceiue.

640

I trowe you shall se, moze knaues come to me,

Whiche when so euer they doo:

They shall haue their meed, as they deserue in deed,

As you shall se shoztly these two.

When they doo pzetend, to haue a good end,

Mark wel then what shall insue:

A bag and a bottle, oz els a rope knottle,

This shall they pzooue to true.

But mark wel this game, I se this geer frame,

C.iii.

Lo

Lo who commeth now in the...

It is Cuthart cutpurse and Pierce pickpurse,
Giue roum now a little cast.

Heere entreth Cutbart cutpurse and Pierce pickpurse, Cut-
hart cutpurse must haue in his hand a purse of money or coun-
ters in it, and a knife in one hand and a whetstone in the o-
ther, and Pierce must haue money or counters in his hand &
gingle it as hee commeth in.

By gogs wounds it dooth me good to the hart,
To se how clenly I plaid this part,
While they stood thrusting together in the throng:
I began to go them among,
And with this knife whiche heer you doo se:
I cut away this purse clenly.

Se to your purses my masters and be ruled by me,
For knaues are abrode therfore beware:
you are warnd and ye take not heed I doo not care.

And also so soon as I had espide,
A woman in the throng whose purse was fate,
I took it by the stringes and clenly it tide,
She knew no more of it then gib our cat,
yet at the last she hied apace,
And said that the money in my hand she saw:
Thou whore said I, I wil haue an action of the case,
And seing thou saist so I wil try the law.

How saist thou Pierce pickpurse art thou not agreed,
These two booties equally to deuide:

Then let vs count the totall sum:
And deuide it equally when we haue doon:

My masters heer is a good fellow y would fain haue some.
What Nichol newfangle be you heer,
So God help me, I am glad with all my hart:

Then

Then ere we depart we wil haue some cheer,
 And of this bootie you shall haue your part.

I thank you bothe euen hartely,
 And I wil doo somewhat for you by and by:
 Are not you two sworn brothers in euery bootie?

Yes that we are truly.

Then can I tel you newes whiche you doo not knowe:
 Suche newes as wil make you ful glad I trowe,
 But first tel me this Pierce pickpurse :
 Whether is the elder, thou or Cutbert cutpurse?

In faith I think we are bothe of one age wel nie,

I suppose there is no great difference truly:
 But wherfore aske you, I pray you tel me why?

I wil tel you the cause without any delay:
 For a peece of land is fallen as I hear say,
 Whiche by succession must come to one of you:
  proper plat it is this is moste true.
 For thou Cutbell tut purse wast Cutbert tht throtes lowe
 And thou Pierce pickpurse by that time thou hast done.
 Canst deriue thy petigree from an auncient house:
 Thy father was Tom theef and thy mother Tib loure.
 This peece of land wherto you inheritours are :
 Is called the land of the two legged mare,
 In whiche peece of ground there is a mare in deed :
 Whiche is the quickest mare in England for speed,
 Therfore if you wil come anon vnto me :
 I wil put you in possession and that you shall se.

I cannot beleeue that suche luck is hapned to vs :

It is true that I to you doo discusse:

If you wil help vs to this peece of ground,
 Bothe of vs to you shall think our selues bound:

Yes in faith you shall haue it you may beleeue me :
 I wil be as good as my woord as shortly you shall se.

                    C.iiii.   Then

¶Then bꝛother Pierce we may think our selues happy,
That euer we were with him acquainted.
¶Euen so we may of a certaintie,
That suche good luck vnto vs hath happened.
But bꝛother Cutbert is it not best,
To go in foꝛ a while and distribute this bootie ꞓ
720
Where as we thꝛee wil make some feast,
And quasse together and be mery.
¶What say you Nichol? I doo agree.

¶Héer entreth in Uertuous liuing.

¶But soft a while be ruled by me,
Look yonder a little doo you not se
Who cometh yonder, a while we wil abide,
Let him say his pleasure and we wil stand aside.
730
¶Oh gratious God how wonderful are thy wooꝛks,
How highly art thou of all men to be pꝛaysed:
Of Chꝛistians, Sarasens, Iewes and also Turks,
Thy gloꝛy ought to be erected and raysed.
What ioyes hast thou pꝛepared foꝛ the verteous life,
And suche as haue thy name in loue and in awe:
Thou hast pꝛomised saluation, to man, childe and wife,
That thy pꝛecepts obserue and keep wel thy law.
And to the verteous life what dooth insue,
Virtutis premium honor Tully dooth say :
740
Honour is the guerdon foꝛ vertue due,
And eternall saluation at the latter day.
How cleer in conscience is the verteous life,
The vicious hath consciences so heauy as lead :
Their conscience and their dooing is alway at strife,
And all though they liue: yet to sin they are dead.
¶God giue you good moꝛowe sir, how doo you to day,
¶God blesse you also bothe now and alway.
I pꝛay you with me haue you any acquaintance ꞓ
yea

88

Yea mary I am an olde freend of yours perchaunce.

If it be so I maruel very muche.
That the dulnes of my wit should be suche:
That you should be altogether out of my memory,
Tel me your name I pray you hartely.
By the faith of my body you wil appose me by an by.
But in faith I was but little when I was first born:
And my mother to tel me my name thought it scorn.

I wil neuer acquaint me with suche in any place:
As are ashamed of their names by gods grace.

I remember my name now it is come to my minde:
I haue mused muche before I could it finde,
Nichol newfangle it is I am your olde freend.

My freend, mary I doo thee defy:
And all suche company I doo deny.
For thou art a companion for roysters and ruffians,
And not fit for any vertuous companions.

And in faith art thou at plain defiance:
Then I se I must go to myne olde acquaintance.
Wel Cutbart cutpurse & pickpurse, we must go together:
For like wil to like quoth the Deuil to the Colier.

In deed thou saist true, it must needs be so:
For like wil euer to his like go.
And my conditions and thine so far doo disagree:
That no familiaritie between vs may be
For thou nurishest vice bothe day and night:
My name is verteous life and in vertue is my delight.
So vice and vertue cannot together be vnited:
But the one the other bath alwaies spighted.
For as water quencheth fire and the flame dooth suppres
So vertue hateth vice and seketh a redres.

Tushe if he be so daungerous let vs not hiim esterm,
And he is not for our company I se very wel:

D.i.   for

Yea merry I am an olde friend of yours
perchaunce

89

...ye be so holy as ye dooth seem, ✠
We and he differ asmuche as heauen and hel.

¶You knowe that like wil to likealway,
And you se how holily he is now bent:
To seek his company why do we assay?
I promise you doo you what you wil, I doo not consent.
For I passe not for him be he better or be he wurse,
¶Freend if you be wise beware your purse.

790 For this fellowe may doo you good when all comes to all:
If you chaunce to lose your purse in cut purse hall.
But in faith fare ye wel, sith of our company you be wery:
We wil go to a place where we wil be mery.
For I se your company and oures doo far differ:
For like wil to like quoth the Deuil to the Colier.

¶Wel let vs be gone and bid him adue:
For I se this prouerb prooueth very true.

¶Then let vs go to Hob filchers house:
Where we wil be mery and quasse carouse.

800 And there shall we finde Tom tospot with other mo:
Meet mates for vs therfore let vs go.

¶Then seeing we are all of one minde: Exeunt
Let vs three go and leaue a braue heer behinde. they sing

¶They sing this song as they go out from the place.
¶God ostis lay a crab in the fire and broil a messe of souse a:
That wee may tosse the bole to and fro, & brinks them all carouse a.
¶And I wil pledge Tom tospot til I be as drunk as a mouse a:
Who so wil drinke to me all day, I wil pledge them all carouse a.
¶Then we wil not spare for any cost, so long as we be in house a:

810 Then ostis fil the pot again, for I pledge them all carouse a. ¶Finis.

¶Oh wicked imps that haue suche delight,
In euil conuersation wicked and abhominable:
And from vertues lore withdrawe your selues quite,
And lean to vice moste vile and detestable,
How prone and redy we are vice to ensue:

How

✠ For if he be so holy as he dooth seem,

How dere we be good councel to heare?
How strauge we make it our harts to renue:
How little we haue Gods threats in feare:

で he this is spo
ke he must pause
a while & then say
as followeth.

Saint Augustine saith in his v. book de ciuitate Dei,
Coniunctæ sunt ædes Virtutis et Honoris: saith he:
The houses of vertue and Honour ioyned together be,
And so the way to honours house is disposed,
That through vertues house he must needs passe :
Or els from honour he shall soon be deposed,
And brought to that point that he before was.
　　But if through vertue, honour be attained:
　　The path to saluation may soon be gayned.
Some there be that doo fortune prefer,
Some esteem plesure more then verteous life :
But in my opinion all suche doo er,
For vertue and fortune be not at strife.
　　Where vertue is, fortune must needs growe:
　　But fortune without vertue hath soon the ouerthrowe
Thrise happy are they that doo vertue embrace,
For a crown of glory shall be their reward:
Sathan at no time may him any thing deface,
For God ouer him wil haue suche regard,
　　That his foes he shall soon tread vnder foot :
　　And by Gods permission pluck them vp by the root.
It booteth not vice against vertue to stur,
For why vice is feeble and of no force :
But Virtus eterna preclaraque habetur.
Wherfore I would all men would haue remorse,
　　And eschue euil company bile and pernitious :
　　Delight in vertuous men and hate the vicious.
And as the end of vertue is honour and felicitie,
So mark wel the end of wickednes and vice:
Shame in this world and pain eternally,
　　　　D. ii.　　　　　　　　　　Wherfore

820

830

840

+ wherefore you that are here learn to be wise,
And the end of the one with the other way:
By that time you haue heard the end of this play.

But why doo I thus muche say in the praise of vertue,
Sith the thing praise worthy needs no praise at all:
It praiseth it self sufficiently this is true,
Whiche chaseth away sin as bitter as gall:
And where vertue is, it need not to be praysed | Intrat
For the renown therof shall soon be raysed. | good fame.

¶Oh verteous life God rest you mercy,
To you am I come for to attend:
¶Good fame ye are welcome hartely,
I pray you who did you hither send?
¶Euen Gods promise hath sent me vnto you,
Willing me from you not to depart:
But alwayes to giue attendance due,
And in no wise from you to start.
For God of his promise hath moste liberally,
Sent me Good fame to you Uertuous life:
Wherby it may be seen manifestly,
Gods great zeal to vertue bothe in man and wife.
For why they may be sure that I good fame,
From the verteous life wil neuer stray:
Wherby honour and renown may growe to their name,
And eternall saluation at the latter day.
¶God is gratious and ful of great mercy,
To suche as in vertue set their whole delight:
Powring his benefits on them abundantly,
Oh man what meanest thou with thy sauiour to fight?
Come vnto him for he is ful of mercy,
The fountain of vertue and of godlines the spring:
Come vnto him and thou shalt liue euerlastingly,
He dooth not require thee any price to bring,

Venite

+ wherefore you that are here learn to be wise,

Venite ad me omnes qui laboratis et onerati estis et
ego refossilabo vos.

Come vnto me ye that trauail (saith he)
And suche as with sin are heuely loden:
And of me my self refreshed you shall be,
Repent, repent, your sinnes shalbe down troden.
Wel good fame sith God of his goodnes,
Hath hether sent you on me to attend: 890
Let vs giue thank to him with humblenes,
And perswade with all men their liues to amend.

¶ Verteous life I doo therto agree,
For it becommeth all men for to doo so:
But beholde yonder cometh Gods promise as seemeth me,
And Honour with him commeth also.

Intrat Gods pro-
mise and Ho-
nour with him.

¶ Suche godly company pleaseth me very wel:
For vicio⁹ mē frō our cōpany we should expel

¶ God rest you mery bothe and God be your guide:
¶ We are now come to the place where we must abide, 900
For from you verteous life I honour may not slide.

¶ I am Gods promise whiche is a thing etern,
And nothing more surer then his promise may be:
A sure foundation to suche as wil learn,
Gods precepts to obserue, then must they needs se.
Honour in this world and at last a crown of glory:
Euer in ioy and mirth and neuer to be sory.
Wherfore oh verteous life, to you we doo repair,
As messengers from God his promise to fulfil:
And therfore sit you down now in this chair, 910
For to ēdue you with honour it is Gods promise and wil.

¶ Vertuous liuing sitteth down in the chair.

¶ Now take this swoord in hand as a token of victory,
This crown from my hed to you I shall giue:
I crown you with it as one moste worthy,

D.iii.

And

93

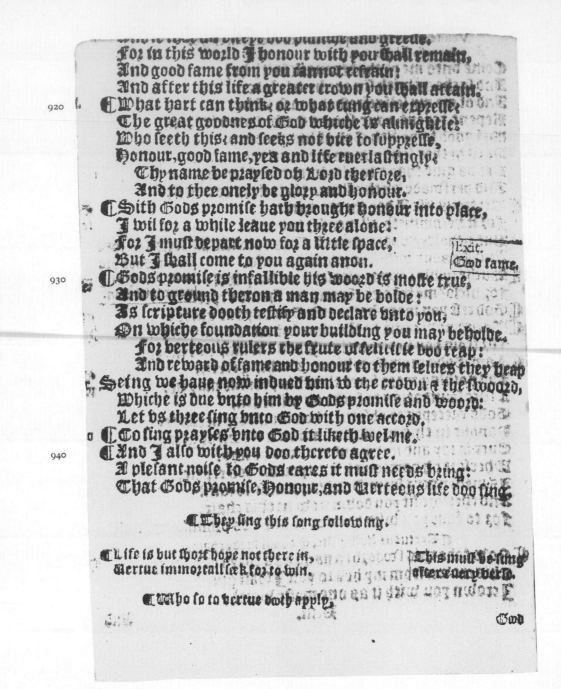

For in this world I honour with you shall remain,
And good fame from you cannot refrain:
And after this life a greater crown you shall attain.

920 ¶What hart can think, or what tung can expresse,
The great goodnes of God whiche is almightie?
Who seeth this, and seeks not vice to suppresse,
Honour, good fame, yea and life everlastingly?
Thy name be praysed oh Lord therfore,
And to thee onely be glory and honour.

¶Sith Gods promise hath brought honour into place,
I wil for a while leaue you three alone:
For I must depart now for a little space,
But I shall come to you again anon.

Exit.
God fame.

930 ¶Gods promise is infallible his woord is moste true,
And to ground theron a man may be bolde:
As scripture dooth testify and declare vnto you,
On whiche foundation your building you may beholde.
For verteous rulers the frute of felicitie doo reap:
And reward of fame and honour to them selues they heap
Seeing we haue now indued him w the crown & the swoord,
Whiche is due vnto him by Gods promise and woord:
Let vs three sing vnto God with one accord.

¶To sing prayses vnto God it liketh wel me.
940 ¶And I also with you doo thereto agree.
A plesant noise, to Gods eares it must neds bring:
That Gods promise, Honour, and Verteous life doo sing.

¶They sing this song following.

¶Life is but short hope not there in,   This must be sung
Vertue immortall seek for to win.   after euery verse.

¶Who so to vertue doth apply,

God

Good fame and honour shall obtain, †

And also liue eternally,

For verteous life this is the gain,

    Life is but. &c.

Gods promise sure wil neuer fail,

    His holy wordis a perfect grounde

The fort of Vertue ob man assail,

    Where treasure alwayes doth abound,

        Life is but. &c.

To thée alone be laud and praise,

    Oh Lord that art so merciful,

Who neuer failed at all assaies,

    To ayd and help the pitiful.

        Life is but. &c.   Exeunt omnes.

        Finis.

Heer entreth in Nichol newfangle, and bringeth in with him a bag, a staffe, a bottle, and two halters, going about the place shewing it vnto the audience and singeth this:

Trim marchandice trim trim, trim marchandice trim trim.

    Hée may sing this as oft as hée thinketh good.   N

Mary heer is marchandice who so list for to buy any

Come se for your loue and buy for your money,

This is land whiche I must distribute anon,

According to my promise or I begon,

For why Tom tospot since he went hence,

Hath increased a noble iust vnto nine pence,

And Raphe roister it may no other wise be holen,

Hath brought a pack of wull to a fair pair of halen,

This is good thrift sirs learn it who shall:

And now a couple of felowes are come from cutpurse hall,

And there haue they brought many a purse to wrack,

Lo heer is geer wll make their necks for to crack,

        D.iiii.   161

+ Good fame and honour must obtaine

Lo heer it is redy in my right hand
A wallet and a bottle, but it is not to be solde:
I tolde them before that of beggers maner it did holde.
And for Cutbart cutpurs & Pierce pickpurs heer is good
This is the land of the two legged mare.   (fare
Whiche I to them promised & deuide it with discretion:
Shortly you shall se I wil put them in possession.
How like you this marchandise my masters? is it not trim
A wallet, a bottle, a staffe and a string:
How saist thou wat waghalter is not this a trim thinge
In faith Rafe roister is in good case as I suppose:
For he hath lost all that he hath saue his doublet & his hose
And Tom tospot is euen at that same point:
For he would loose a lim or ieobard a ioint.
But beholde yonder they come bothe, now all is goist and
I knowe their erand and what is their intent.   (spent

Ther entreth in Raphe Royster & Tom Tospot in their Doublet and their Hose, and no Cap nor Hat on their hed, sauing a
night cap because the stringes of the beards may not be seen, &
Raphe roister must curse and ban as he commeth in.

¶Wel be as be may is no banning.
But I fear that when that this gear shall come to scanting
The land to the whiche we did wholy trust:
Shall be gone from vs and we cast in the dust.
¶Gogs blood if Nichol newfangle serue vs so:
We may say that we haue had a shrewd blowe,
For all that I had is now lost at the dice:
My swoord my buckler, and all at sink and cise.
My cote, my cloke, and my hat also:
And now in my doublet and my hose I am fain to go.
Therfore if Nichol newfangle help not now at a pinche

For I promisd Tom Tospot and Rafe royster a piece of land

I am vndoon foz of land I haue not an inche.

℃ By gogs wounds euen so is it now with me:

   I am in my doublet and my hosen as you se.

   Foz all that I had dooth lie at pledge foz ale:

   By the masse I am as bare as my naile.

   Not a crosse of money to blesse me haue I:

   But I trowe we shall meet Nichol newfangle by and by.

℃ Turn hether, turn hether, I say sir knaue:

   Foz I am euen he that you so fain would haue.

℃ What: master Nichol: are you heer all this while: 1020

℃ I think I am heer oz els I doo thee begile.

℃ So God help me I am glad that you be in sight:

   Foz in faith your pzesence hath made my hart light.

℃ I wil make it lighter anon I trowe:

   My masters I haue a peece of land foz you, doo you not

℃ Mary that is the cause of our hether resozt: (knowe:

   Foz now we are void of all ioy and comfozt.

℃ You se in what care we now stand in:

   And you heard vs also euen now I ween.

   Wherfoze good master Nichol let vs haue this land now: 1030

   And we shall think our selues muche bound vnto you.

℃ You knowe that I this land must deuide,

   Whiche I shall doo but a while abide.

   All thy goods foz Ale at pledge be,

   And thou saist a pair of Dice haue made thee free.

   First Rafe roister come thou vnto me.

   Because thou hast lost euery whit at Dice:

   Take ȳ this bag to cary bzead and cheese.

   And take thou this bottle and mark what I shall say: 1040

   If he chaunce to eat the bzead and cheese by the way.

   Doo thou in this matter followe my councel:

   Dzink vp the dzink and knock him about the hed with the

   And because that Rafe is the elder knaue: (bottle.

He giueth the bag to R. R. and the bottle to T. T.

              T. t.   He

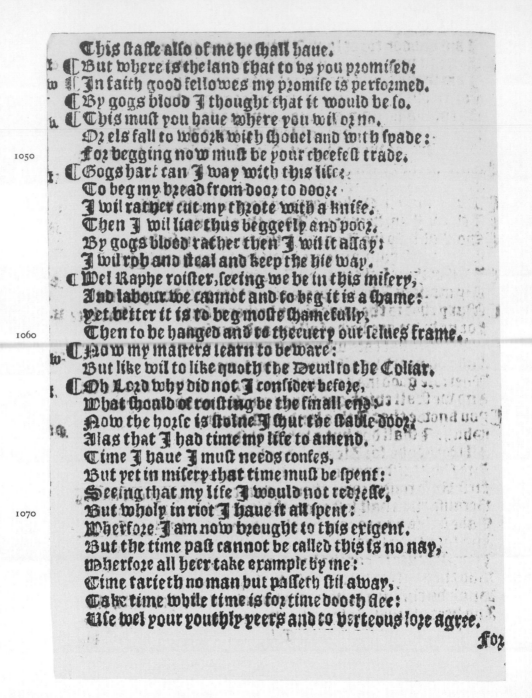

This staffe also of me he shall haue.

¶ But where is the land that to vs you promisede

¶ In faith good fellowes my promise is performed.

¶ By gogs blood I thought that it would be so.

¶ This must you haue where you wil or no,

Or els fall to woork with shouel and with spade:

For begging now must be your cheefest trade.

¶ Gogs hart can I way with this life,

To beg my bread from door to door,

I wil rather cut my throte with a knife,

Then I will liue thus beggerly and poor,

By gogs blood rather then I wil it assay:

I wil rob and steal and keep the hie way.

¶ Wel Raphe roister, seeing we be in this misery,

And labour we cannot and to beg it is a shame:

Yet better it is to beg moste shamefully,

Then to be hanged and to theeuery our selues frame.

¶ Now my maisters learn to beware:

But like wil to like quoth the Deuil to the Coliar.

¶ Oh Lord why did not I consider before,

What should of roisting be the small end

Now the horse is stolne I shut the stable door,

Alas that I had time my life to amend.

Time I haue I must needs confes,

But yet in misery that time must be spent:

Seeing that my life I would not redresse,

But wholy in riot I haue it all spent:

Wherfore I am now brought to this exigent.

But the time past cannot be called this is no nay,

Wherfore all heer take example by me:

Time tarieth no man but passeth stil away,

Take time while time is for time dooth flee:

Use wel your youthly yeers and to verteous lore agree.

For

For if I to vertue had any respect,
This misfortune to me could not have chaunced:
But because vnto vice I was a subiect.
To no good fame may I be now aduaunced, 1080
My credit also is now quite staunched.
Wherfore I would all men my woful care might se:
That I to them a mirrour might be.

℄ Oh all ye parents to you I doo say,
Haue respect to your children and for their education:
Lest you answer therfore at the latter day,
And your meed shalbe eternall damnation.
If my parents had brought me vp in vertue and learning,
I should not haue had this shameful end:
But all licenciously was my vp bringing, 1090
Wherfore learn by me your faults to amend:
But neither in vertue, learning, or yet honest trade,
Was I bred vp my liuing for to get:
Therfore in misery my time away must bade,
For vicious persons beholde now the net.
I am in the snare I am caught with the gin:
And now it is to late I cannot again begin.

℄ This geer would haue been seen to before,
But now my masters you are on the score, 1100
Be packing I say and get you hence,
Learn to say I pray good master giue me nine pence.

℄ Thou villain art onely the causer of this wo:
Therfore thou shalt haue some what of me or ere I go.

℄ Thou hast giuen me a bottle heer:
But thou shalt drink first of it be it ale or bier.

℄ Raphe royster beateth him with his staffe, and Tom Tospot
with his bottle.

℄ Take this of me before I go hence,
℄ Take that of me in part of recompence.

E.ii.

Now

99

Now am I oziuen to play the matter of feule.
Come no neer me you knaues foz your life.
Lest I stick you bothe with this woodknife.

They haue him
down & beat hi, &
he crieth foz help

Back I say, back thou sturdy begger:
Body of me they haue tane away my dagger

Now in faith you whozsone take heed I you aduice:
How you doo any moze yung men entice.

Now fare wel thou hast thy iust meed:

Now we go a begging God send vs good speed.

1120

Raphe royster and Tom tolpot go out and Seueritis the
Iudge entreth, and Nichol Newfangle lieth on the ground
groning.

That vpzight iudgement without parcialitie,
Be ministred duly to il dooers and offenders:
I am one whose name is Seueritie,
Appointed a Iudge to suppzesse euil dooers.
Not foz hatred noz yet foz malice:
But to aduaunce vertue and suppzesse vice.
Wherfoze Ysodorus these woozds dooth say,

Non est Iudex si in eo non est Iusticia:

1130

He is not a Iudge that Iustice dooth want,
But he that truthe and equitie dooth plant,
Tully also these woozds dooth expzesse:
Whiche woozds are very true doutlesse.

Semper iniquus est Iudex, qui aut inuidet aut fauet.

They are vnrightful Iudges all:
That are eyther enuyous oz els partiall.

Help me vp good sir foz I haue got a fall.

What cause haue you my freend thus heuely to grone.

Oh sir I haue good cause to make great mone.

1140

Heer were to fellowes but right now:
That I think haue killed me I make God avow.
I pzay you tel me am I aliue oz am I dead:

fellowe

Fellowe it is moze meet foz thee to be in thy bed,
Then to lie heer in suche sozt as thou doost.

In faith I should haue laid some of the knaues in the dust
If I had had your swoozd right now in pzesence:
I would haue had a leg oz an arme ere they had gone héce

Who is it that hath doon thee this iniury?

A couple of beggers haue doon me this villany.

I se if seueritie should not be executed,
One man should not liue by another:
If suche iniuries should not be confuted,
The childe would regard neither father noz mother.
Giue me thy hand and I shall help thee:

Holde fast your swoozd then I pzay you hartely. He riseth.

Now freend it appeereth vnto me.
That you haue been a trauailer of the countrie,
And suche as trauail doo hear of thinges done:
Alwel in the cuntrie as the cittie of London.
How say you my freend can you tel any newes?

That can I, foz I came lately from the stewes.
There are knaues abzode you may beleeue me:
As in this place shoztly you shall se.
No moze woozds but mum & stād a while aside:
Yonder commeth two knaues therfoze abide.

Intrat C. cutpurs and P. pickpurse.

By gogs wounds if he help not now we are vndone:
By the masse foz my part I wot not whether to run,
we be so pursude on euery side:
That by gogs hart I wot not where to abide.
Euery Constable is charged to make pziuy serche:
So ÿ if we may begot, we shalbe thzowen ouer the perche.

If Nichol newfangle help vs not now in our need,
We are like in our business ful euil to speed.
Therfoze let vs make no delay:

C. iij.   But

But seek him out of hand and be gone away.

ew ℭ Soft my masters a while I you pray.
For I am heer for whom you doo seek:
For yourknowe that like wil neuer from like:
I promised you of late a pece of land:
Whiche by and by shall fall into your hand.

℺ What master Nichol how doo you to day?

k. ℺ For the passion of God master Nichol help to rid vs away
And help vs to the land where of you did say.
That we might make money of it vp an by:
For out of the realme we purpose to flee.

ew ℭ Mary I wil help you I swear by all halowes:
And wil not part from you til you come to the Galowes.
Lo noble Seueritie these be they without dout,
On whom this rumor of theenery is gone about,
Therfore my masters heer is the snare:
That shall lead you to the land called the two legged mare.

℺ He putteth about eche of their necks
a halter.

ity ℭ My freend holde them fast euen in that plight:
ew ℭ Then come and help me with your swoord for I fear they
ity ℭ Striue not my masters for it shall not auail: (wil fight,
But a while giue ear vnto my counsail.
Your owne woords hath condemned you for to die:
Therfore to God make your selues redy.
And by and by I wil send one whiche for your abusion,
Shall lead you to the place of execution.

ew ℭ Help to tie their hāds before ye be gone. |He helpeth to tie the[m
ity ℭ Now they are bound I wil send one to you anon.   Exit.
ew ℭ Ah my masters how like you this play,
You shall take possession of your land to day.
I wil help to bridle the two legged mare,
And bothe you for to ride need not to spare.

Now

Now so God help me I swear by this bread:
I maruail who shall play the knaue when you twain be
                                                   (dead. C.c

❡ Oh cursed caytiue borne in an euil houre,
Wo vnto me that euer I did thee knowe:
For of all iniquitie thou art the bowre,
The seed of Sathan thou doost alwayes sowe,
Thou onely hast giuen me the ouerthrowe.
Wo worth the houre wherin I was borne,
Wo worthe the time that euer I knew thee,
For now in misery I am forlorn,
Oh all youth take example by me.
Flee from euil company, as from a serpent you would flee
For I to you all a mirrour may be.
I haue been daintely and delicately bred,
But nothing at all in verteous lore:
And now I am but a man dead,
Hanged I must be whiche greeueth me ful sore,
Note wel the end of me therfore,
And you that Fathers and Mothers be:
Bring not vp your children in to muche libertie.

❡ Sith that by the law we are now condemned,
Let vs call to God for his mercy and his grace:
And exhort that all vice may be amended,
While we in this world haue time and space.
And though our liues haue licentiously been spent,
Yet at the last to God let vs call:
For he heareth suche as are redy forepent,
And desireth not that sinners should fall:
Now are we ready to suffer come when it shall.

        ❡ Heer entreth in Hankin hangman.
❡ Come Hankin hangman let vs two cast lots:
And between vs deuide a couple of cotes,
Take thou the one and the other shalbe mine.
              C.iiii.

Come, Hankin hangman thou camſt in good time.

They take of the cotes and deuide them.

ſg. ❡Thou ſhouldſt haue one Nichol I ſwear by the maſſe,
   ſoz thou bzingeſt woozk foz me daily to paſſe.
   And thzough thy means I get moze cotes in one yeer,
   Then all my liuing is woozth beſide I ſwear.
   Therfoze Nichol newfangle we wil depart neuer:
   ſoz like wil to like quoth the Deuil to the Colier.

1250   ew ❡Now farwel Hankin hangman: farwel to thee:

ſg. ❡farwel Nichol newfangle, come you two with mee.

Hankin goeth out and leadeth the one in his right hand, and th[e]
other in his left, hauing halters about their necks.

ew ❡Ha, ha, ha, there is a bzace of hounds, wel woozth a dozen
   Beholde the huntſman leadeth away: (crownes
   I think in twentie townes, on hilles & eke on downes,
     They taken haue their pzay.
   So wel liked was their hunting on hil & eke on mountai[n]
   That now they be vp in a leace:

1260
   To keep with in a ſtring, is it not a gay thing,
     Doo all you holde your peace?
   Why then good gentle boy, how likeſt thou this play?
   No moze but ſay thy minde :
   I ſwear by this day, if thou wilt this aſſay,
     I wil to thee be kinde.
   This is wel bzougbt to paſſe, of me I ſwear by the maſſe.
   Some to hang and other ſome to beg :
   I would I had Balams aſſe, to cary me where I was,
     How ſay you little Meg.

1270
   Raphe roiſter & Tom toſpot, are now not woozth a grote
   So wel with them it is :
   I would I had a pot, foz now I am ſo whot,
     By the maſſe I muſt go piſſe.
   Philip flemming and Haunce, haue daunſt a pzetie daunce
                                   That

And now a great mischaunce, came on while they did
They lie sick of the gout. (praunce.

And in a spittle house, with little Laurence louce,
They be fain for to dwel:
If they eat a morsel of souce, or els a rosted mouce,   1280
They think they doo fare wel.

But as for Peter pickpurse, and also Cutbart cutpurse,
Yow saw them bothe right now :
With them it is muche wurse, for they doo ban and curse,
For the halter shall them bowe.

Now if I had my nag, to se the world wag,
I would straight ride about :
Sinks doo fil the bag, I would not passe a rag,
To hit you on the snout.

℣The Deuil entreth.   1290

℣Ho ho ho mine owne boy make no more delay?   Lu
But leap vp on my back straight way.
℣Then who shall holde my strop while I go to horse?   N
℣Tushe for that doo thou not force.   Lu
Leap vp I say leap vp quickly.
℣Who ball who, and I wil come by an by.   N

Now for a pair of spurres I would giue a good grote:
To try whether this Jade doo amble or trot.
Farwel my masters til I come again,
For now I must make a iourney into spain.   1300
        He rideth away on the Deuils back.

        ℣Heer entreth Uerteous life and Honour.

℣Oh worthy diademe, oh iewel moste precious,
Oh vertue whiche doost all worldly things excel:
How worthy a treasure thou art to the verteous:
Thy praise no pen may write nor no tung tel.
For I who am called verteous life,
        f.i.   Haue

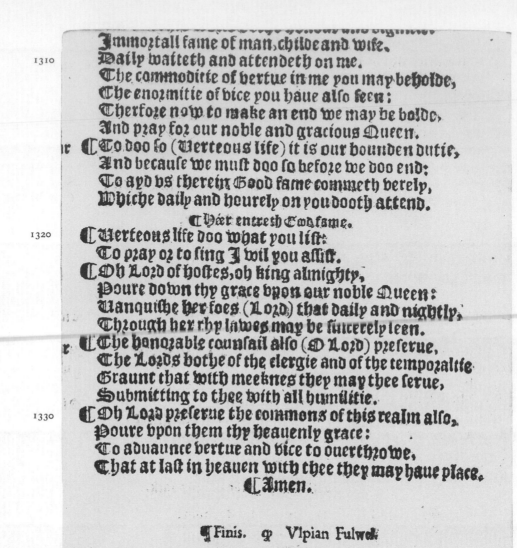

Immortall fame of man, childe and wife,
Daily waiteth and attendeth on me.
The commoditie of vertue in me you may beholde,
The enormitie of vice you haue also seen:
Therfore now to make an end we may be bolde,
And pray for our noble and gracious Queen.

¶To doo so (Verteous life) it is our bounden dutie,
And because we must doo so before we doo end:
To ayd vs therein Good fame commeth verely,
Whiche daily and hourely on you dooth attend.

¶Héer entreth Godsfame.

¶Verteous life doo what you list,
To pray or to sing I wil you assist.

¶Oh Lord of hostes, oh king almighty,
Poure down thy grace vpon our noble Queen:
Vanquishe her foes (Lord) that daily and nightly,
Through her thy lawes may be sincerely seen.

¶The honorable counsail also (O Lord) preserue,
The Lords bothe of the clergie and of the temporalite
Graunt that with meeknes they may thee serue,
Submitting to thee with all humilitie.

¶Oh Lord preserue the commons of this realm also,
Poure vpon them thy heauenly grace:
To aduaunce vertue and vice to ouerthrowe,
That at last in heauen with thee they may haue place.

¶Amen.

¶Finis. ⚭ Vlpian Fulwel

¶ Where like to like is matched so,
That vertue must of force decay:
There God with vengeance, plagues and wo,
By iudgement iust must néeds repay.
　　For like to like the worldlings crye
　　Although bothe likes dw grace defy.

¶ And where as Sathan planted hath,
In vicious mindes a sinful trade:
There like to like dw walke his path,
By whiche to him like they are made.
　　So like with like reward obtain:
　　To haue their méed in endles pain.

¶ Like wise in faith where matches bée,
And where as God hath planted grace:
There dw his children stil agrée,
And like to like dw run their race.
　　Like Christe, like harts, of Christian men:
　　As like to like wel coupled then.

¶ Thorfore like grace, like faith and loue,
Like vertue springes in eche degrée:
Where like assistance from aboue,
Dwth make them like so right to bée.
　　A holy God, a Christe moste iust:
　　And so like soules in him to trust.

¶ Then like as Christe aboue dwth reign,
In heauen hie our sauiour best:
So like with him shalbe our gain,
In peace and ioy and endles rest.
　　If wée our selues like him dw frame:
　　In fear of his moste holy name.

¶ To him be praise that grace dwth giue,
Wherby he fashioneth vs a new:
And makes vs holily to liue,
Like to him self in faith moste true.
　　Whiche our redemption sure hath wrought
　　Like him to be moste déerly bought.

　　　　　　　　　¶ Finis

1340

1350

1360

1370

1. Readings in Q1 affected by cropping, binding, and damage to the paper. Some speech headings, which have been lost completely, can be deduced from the action of the play. Doubtful ones are preceded by a question mark. Q2 is noted in support, where applicable.

2 ⟨L⟩ike   3 ⟨ry⟩godly   25 ⟨❡ The prologue.⟩

31 ⟨A⟩nd   33 ⟨W⟩ith   35 ⟨M⟩erely

36 ⟨T⟩he   37 ⟨I⟩s   39 ⟨O⟩ur

40 ⟨A⟩s   42 ⟨h⟩eer   43 ⟨T⟩he

45 ⟨Y⟩ou   48 ⟨T⟩he   49 ⟨A⟩nd

51 ⟨S⟩ome   52 ⟨O⟩ther   53 ⟨T⟩o

54 ⟨W⟩herfore   55 ⟨D⟩esiring

58 ⟨And the Deuil with the Coliar the theef that seeks ẏ theef,⟩

63 hath⟨a⟩   64 of⟨⁖⟩   66 ⟨Mi. M⟩ew

90 catchword An⟨d⟩   91 ⟨And especially breeches as big as good barels.⟩

110 L⟨ucifer⟩   111 M⟨i. New⟩   112 L⟨ucifer⟩

113 M⟨i. New⟩   114 L⟨ucifer⟩   115 M⟨i. New⟩

123 ⟨But I am like to cary the mark to my graue.⟩   124 ⟨Luci⟩fr

128 ⟨Mi. M⟩ew   132 ⟨Lucife⟩r   144 ⟨Mi. Ne⟩w

148 ⟨Lucifer⟩   152 ⟨Mi. Ne⟩w   153 ⟨Lucife⟩r

159 Mi.⟨New⟩   160 Lu⟨cifer⟩   161 Mi⟨New⟩

163 Lu⟨cifer⟩   165 Mi.⟨New⟩   169 Lu⟨cifer⟩

171 Mi.⟨New⟩   178 C.⟨Coliar⟩   179 Mi⟨. New⟩

180 C.⟨Coliar⟩   182 Mi⟨. New⟩   183 C.⟨Coliar⟩

184 Mi⟨. New⟩   186 C.⟨Coliar⟩   188 Mi⟨. New⟩

189 ⟨Tel me what market thou hast made of thy coles to day.⟩

190 ⟨C. Co⟩l.   194 ⟨Mi. M⟩ew   195 ⟨C. Col⟩iar

199 ⟨Mi. M⟩ew   202 ⟨Lucife⟩r   taket⟨h⟩

203 ⟨C. Co⟩l.   hã⟨d.⟩   204 ⟨Lucife⟩r

205 ⟨Mi. M⟩ew   hel⟨?⟩   206 ⟨Lucife⟩r

207 ⟨C. Co⟩l.   208 ⟨Mi. M⟩ew   209 ⟨Lucife⟩r

210 ⟨Mi. M⟩ew   211 in⟨ : ⟩   213 daũc⟨e⟩

222 ⟨S⟩ith   228 M⟨i. New⟩   232 C.⟨Coliar⟩

233 L⟨ucifer⟩   234 M⟨i. New⟩   236 L⟨ucifer⟩

237 M⟨i. New⟩   240 L⟨ucifer⟩   243 M⟨i. New⟩

245 L⟨ucifer⟩   246 M⟨i. New⟩   247 L⟨ucifer⟩

248 M⟨i. New⟩   249 L⟨ucifer⟩   250 M⟨i. New⟩

251 L⟨ucifer⟩   252 M⟨i. New⟩   253 L⟨ucifer⟩

254 M⟨i. New⟩   255 L⟨ucifer⟩

256 ⟨Mi. New   ¶Is there neuer a knaue heer wil keep the deuil company?⟩

270 ⟨C. Tos⟩   272 ⟨Mi. New⟩   274 ⟨C. Tos⟩

284 ⟨Mi. New⟩   288 ⟨C. Tos⟩   290 ⟨Mi. New⟩

292 ⟨C. Tos⟩   293 ⟨Mi. New⟩   294 ⟨C. Tos⟩

296 ⟨Mi. New⟩   297 ⟨T. Tos⟩   299 ⟨Mi. Mew⟩

300 ⟨T. Tos⟩   304 M⟨i. New⟩   312 T⟨. Tos⟩

314 M⟨i. New⟩   319 R.⟨Royst⟩   320 Mi⟨. New⟩

321 T.⟨Tos⟩

322 ⟨R. Royst   ℭGod a mercy good fellowe tel me what thou art.⟩

323 ⟨Mi. Me⟩w   324 ⟨T. To⟩s   325 ⟨R. Roy⟩st

327 ⟨T. To⟩s   329 like⟨:⟩   331 ⟨R. Ro⟩yst.

333 ⟨T. To⟩s   337 ⟨Mi. Me⟩w.   342 ⟨R. Roy⟩st

343 ⟨T. Tos⟩   345 ⟨Mi. Me⟩w   350 ⟨R. Roy⟩st

353 ⟨T. Tos⟩   354 ⟨Mi. Me⟩w   355 ⟨Ye shall se⟩

364 R.⟨Royst⟩   365 T.⟨Tos⟩   366 M⟨i. New⟩

367 B⟨othe⟩   368 M⟨i. New⟩   370 R.⟨Royst⟩

371 M⟨i. New⟩   376 T⟨. Tos⟩   377 R⟨. Royst⟩

378 M⟨i. New⟩   381 R⟨. Royst⟩   382 T⟨. Tos⟩

383 M⟨i. New⟩   386 R⟨. Royst⟩   387 M⟨. New⟩

388 ⟨Now let me hear how⟩   390 Christma⟨s⟩

391 ⟨T. To⟩s   brass⟨e⟩   392 ⟨Mi. M⟩ew

393 ⟨T. T⟩os   397 God⟨,⟩   399 ⟨R. Ro⟩yst

400 ⟨Mi. M⟩ew   401 ⟨R. R⟩oyst   402 ⟨Mi. M⟩ew

403 ⟨R. Ro⟩yst   gard⟨e⟩   409 ⟨Mi. M⟩ew

411 ⟨T. To⟩s   412 ⟨Mi. M⟩ew   413 ⟨T. To⟩s

414 ⟨Mi. N⟩ew   415 ⟨T. To⟩ſ   417 ⟨Mi. Ne⟩w

425 ⟨C⟩I   R. R⟨oyſt⟩   426 ⟨C⟩I   Mi.⟨New⟩

433 ⟨C⟩Then   T. T⟨oſ⟩   445 ⟨C⟩But   Mi.⟨New⟩

446 ⟨C⟩Tuſhe   T. T⟨oſ⟩   455 ⟨Mi. N⟩ew

458 ⟨R. Roi⟩ſt   471 ⟨Mi. N⟩ew   the⟨n⟩

475 ⟨R. Ro⟩iſt   476 ⟨Mi. Ne⟩w

480 ⟨Bothe⟩.   481 ⟨Mi. Ne⟩w   482 ⟨R. Roi⟩ſt

486 ⟨T. To⟩ſ   catchword Com⟨e⟩   487 ⟨Mi. New⟩

495 H⟨aunce⟩   499 N⟨i. New⟩   500 R.⟨Roiſt⟩

501 T.⟨Toſ⟩   503 H⟨aunce⟩   505 N⟨i. New⟩

506 R.⟨Roiſt⟩   507 H⟨aunce⟩   511 R.⟨Roiſt⟩

513 Mi⟨. New⟩   515 T.⟨Toſ⟩   517 ⟨¶⟩Omni   Ha⟨unce⟩

518 Mi.⟨New⟩   520 ⟨Haunc⟩e   522 mas⟨:⟩

524 ⟨T. To⟩ſ   532 ⟨Mi. Ne⟩w   535 ⟨Haunc⟩e

536 ⟨N. N⟩ew   539 ⟨Haunc⟩e   543 ⟨Mi. N⟩ew

547 ⟨T. To⟩ſ.   548 ⟨Haunc⟩e   549 ⟨Mi. N⟩ew

553 ⟨I think⟩   554 H⟨aunce⟩   555 N⟨i. New⟩

557 T.⟨Toſ⟩   562 Mi⟨. New⟩   563 T.⟨Toſ⟩

564 N⟨i. New⟩   568 T.⟨Toſ⟩   571 Mi⟨. New⟩

572 T.⟨Toſ⟩   579 Ph⟨. Flem⟩

585 ⟨What?captain how goeth the world with you?⟩   586 ⟨Mi. Ne⟩w

588 ⟨C. Cut⟩   589 ⟨Ph. Flo⟩m

591 ⟨Mi. Ne⟩w   597 ⟨Ph. Fle⟩m   599 ⟨Haunc⟩e

601 ⟨Mi. Ne⟩w   602 ⟨Haunce⟩   610 ⟨C. Cut⟩

612 ⟨Haunc⟩e   613 ⟨Ph. Fle⟩m   614 ⟨C. Cut⟩

615 ⟨Mi. Ne⟩w.   620 M⟨i. New⟩

650 ⟨Lo who cummeth now in suche haste:⟩   658 ⟨Cutba⟩rt

659 ⟨cutpur⟩se.   664 ⟨Mi. Ne⟩w   667 ⟨Pierce⟩

668 ⟨pickpu⟩rs   675 ⟨Cutba⟩rt   676 ⟨cutpur⟩se.

677 ⟨P. pickpurs⟩.   679 ⟨Mi. Ne⟩w   680 ⟨C. cutpurse⟩

682 P.⟨pickpurs⟩   684 Mi⟨. New⟩   687 B⟨othe⟩

688 Mi⟨. New⟩   692 P.⟨pickpurs⟩   693 C.⟨cutpurse⟩

695 M⟨i. New⟩   698 ⟨A⟩   709 C.⟨cutpurse⟩   710 Mi⟨. New⟩

711 P.⟨pickpurs⟩   713 Mi.⟨New⟩   715 ⟨Cutba⟩rt

716 ⟨cutpur⟩se.   717 ⟨Pierc⟩e   718 ⟨pickpu⟩rs

723 ⟨Cutba⟩rt   724 ⟨cutpur⟩se.   726 ⟨Mi. N⟩ew

730 ⟨Uer. Li⟩.   746 ⟨Mi. N⟩ew   747 ⟨Uer. Li.⟩

749 ⟨Yea mary I am an olde freend of yours perchaunce.   N. New⟩

750 U⟨er. Li.⟩   754 N.⟨New⟩   757 Ue⟨r. Li.⟩

759 Mi⟨. New⟩   762 U⟨er. Li.⟩   766 Mi⟨New⟩

770 Ue⟨r. Li.⟩   780 Pi⟨erce⟩

782 ⟨For if he be so holy as he dooth seem,⟩

784 ?⟨C. Cut⟩ Q2   789 ⟨Mi. Ne⟩w   796 ?⟨P. Pick⟩ Q2

798 ?⟨C. Cut⟩ Q2   802 ?⟨Mi. New⟩ Q2   805 ?⟨C. Cut.⟩ Q2

807 ⟨Mi. New⟩   809 ?⟨P. Pick⟩ Q2   811 ⟨Uer. Li.⟩

816 ⟨Whē this is spo-⟩   850 ⟨Wherfore you that are heer learn to be wise.⟩

859 ⟨Good⟩   860 ⟨fame⟩   861 ⟨Uer. Li⟩.

863 ⟨Good⟩   784 ?⟨fame⟩   875 ⟨Uer. Li.⟩

893 G⟨ood⟩   894 fa⟨me⟩   897 U⟨er. Li.⟩

899 g⟨ods promise⟩   900 h⟨onour⟩   902 G⟨ods⟩

903 p⟨romise⟩   913 h⟨onour⟩

916 ⟨And se that all vicepe doo punishe and greeue.⟩

920 ⟨Uer. Li.⟩   926 ⟨Good⟩   927 ⟨fame⟩

930 ⟨Gods⟩   931 ⟨promis⟩e.   936 ⟨Honou⟩r

939 ⟨Gods Pr⟩o   940 ⟨Uer. Li .⟩

947 ⟨Good fame and honour must obtain:⟩   965 N⟨i. New⟩

979 ⟨For I promised Tom tospot and Rafe roister a peece of land⟩

996 Doub⟨t⟩   998 seen⟨t⟩

1000 ?⟨T. Tos⟩ Q2   1004 ?⟨R. Roist⟩ Q2   1012 T⟨. Tos⟩

1018 N⟨i. New⟩   1020 R.⟨Roist⟩   1021 N⟨i. New⟩

1022 T⟨. Tos⟩   1024 N⟨i. New⟩   1026 R.⟨Roist⟩

1028 T.⟨Tos⟩   1032 Ni⟨. New⟩   1045 ⟨R. Rois⟩t

1046 ⟨Mi. Ne⟩w   1047 ?⟨T. Tos⟩ Q2   1048 ⟨Mi. Ne⟩w

1051 ⟨R. Rois⟩t   1057 ⟨T. Tos⟩   1061 ⟨Mi. Ne⟩w

1063 ⟨R. Roist⟩	1084 T⟨. Tof⟩	1098 N⟨i. New⟩
1102 R.⟨Roist⟩	1104 T.⟨Tof⟩	1108 R.⟨Roist⟩
1109 T.⟨Tof⟩	1110 ⟨Mi. New ¶Now am I driuen to play⟩	
1115 ⟨R. Roy⟩st	1117 ⟨Mi. New⟩	1118 ⟨R. Roy⟩st
1122 ⟨Seueri⟩ty	1137 ⟨Mi. New⟩	1138 ⟨Seuerit⟩y
1139 ⟨Mi. New⟩	1143 S⟨euerity⟩	1145 Mi⟨. New⟩
1148 Se⟨uerity⟩	1149 N⟨i. New⟩	1150 S⟨euerity⟩
1155 N⟨i. New⟩	1156 S⟨euerity⟩	1161 N⟨i. New⟩
1167 C⟨. cutpurse⟩	1173 P.⟨pick.⟩	
1176 ⟨But seek him out of hand⟩		1177 ⟨Mi. N⟩ew
1182 ⟨C. cut⟩.	1183 ⟨P. pic⟩k.	1187 ⟨Mi. N⟩ew
1192 mare⟨.⟩	1195 ⟨Seuer⟩ity	1196 ⟨Mi. Ne⟩w
1197 ⟨Seuer⟩ity	1203 ⟨Mi. Ne⟩w	1204 ⟨Seueri⟩ty
1205 ⟨Mi. Ne⟩w	1211 C. c⟨ut⟩	1229 P.⟨pick⟩
1239 N.⟨New⟩	1244 ⟨H. Han⟩g.	1250 ⟨Mi. Ne⟩w
1251 ⟨H. Han⟩g.	1252 th⟨e⟩	1254 ⟨Mi. Ne⟩w
1255 crownes⟨.⟩	1275 ?⟨That all is now spent out.⟩ Q2	
1291 Lu⟨cifer⟩	1293 Mi⟨. New⟩	1294 Lu⟨cifer⟩
1296 Mi⟨. New⟩	1308 ?⟨Haue in this worlde bothe honour and dignitie.⟩ Q2	
1315 ⟨Honou⟩r	1320 ⟨Good⟩	1321 ⟨fame⟩
1322 ⟨Uer. Li.⟩	1326 ⟨Honou⟩r	1330 ⟨Good⟩
1331 ⟨fame⟩	1336 ⟨¶a song.⟩	

2. Three portions of the text in Q1 are partially illegible because of show-through. The passages concerned are reproduced below. These have been prepared from the photographs of the Bodleian copy, with the show-through removed.

653
¶Heer entreth Cutbart cutpurse and Pierce pickpurse, Cutbart cutpurie muſt haue in his hand a purſe of money oz coũ-
ters in it,and a knife in one hand and a whetſtone in the o-
ther,and Pierce muſt haue money oz counters in his hand &
gingle it as hæ commeth in.

¶By gogs wounds it dooth me good to the hart,
To ſe how clenly I playd this part.

660
While they ſtood thzuſting together in the thzong:
I began to go them among,
And with this knife whiche heer you doo ſe:
I cut away this purſe clenly.
¶Se to your purſes my maſters and be ruled by me,
Foz knaues are abzode therfoze beware:
You are warnd and ye take not heed I doo not care.
¶And alſo ſo ſoon as I had eſpide,
A woman in the thzong whoſe purſe was fat:
I took it by the ſtrings and clenly it vntide,

670
She knew no moze of it then gib our cat.
Yet at the laſt ſhe hied apace,
And ſaid that the money in my hand ſhe ſaw:
Thou whoze ſaid I, I wil haue an action of the cace,
And ſeing thou ſaiſt ſo I wil try the law.
¶How ſaiſt thou Pierce pickpurſe art thoirnot agreed,
Theſe two booties equally to deuiſe
¶Then let vs count the totall ſum:
And deuide it equally when we haue doon
¶My maſters heer is a good fellow ỹ would fain haue ſome.
¶What Nichol new wfangle be you heer.

681
So God help me I am glad with all my han:

116

Here entreth in Nichol newfargle, and bringeth in with him a bag, & 962
staffe, a bottle, and two halters going about the place shewing it unto
the audience and singeth this.

Trim marchandice trim trim, trim marchandice trim trim
Hee may sing this as oft as hee thinketh good.

¶ Mary heer is marchandice who so list for to buy any
Come se for your loue and buy for your money
This is land whiche I must distribute anon
According to my promise or I begon, 970
For why Tom tospot since he went hence?
Hath increased a noble iust vnto nine pence.
And Raphe roister it may no other wise be chosen,
Hath brought a pack of wull to a fair pair of hosen.
This is good thrift sirs learn it who shall:
And now a couple of felowes are come from cutpurse hall
And there haue they brought many a purse to wrack:
Lo heer is geer wil make their necks for to crack, 978

¶ Her entreth in Raphe Roister & Tom Tospot in their Doub- 996
let and their Hose, and no Cap nor Hat on their hed, sauing a
night cap because the stringes of the beards may not be seen &
Raphe roister must curse and ban as he commeth in,

¶ Wel be as be may is no banning, 1000
But I fear that when that this gear shall come to scaning
The land to the whiche we did wholy trust:
Shall be gone from vs and we cast in the dust.
¶ Gogs blood if Nichol newfangle serue vs so:
We may say that we haue had a shrewd blowe.
For all that I had is now lost at the dice:
My swoord my buckler, and all at sink and cise.
My cote, my cloke, and my hat also:
And now in my doublet and my hose I am fain to go.
Therfore if Nichol newfangle help not now at a pinche: 1010

117

3. Doubtful and Irregular Readings.

4 **followeth**]t indistinct   6 **councel**]o small fount

11 **players**] stop raised   14 **Godes**]es added by hand   **pro mifes**

38 **tung**]t damaged   58 [1]**t⟨h⟩e**] hole in paper   61 **it**]t anomalous, or damaged **f**   100 **Héer**]ée a single type, usually has an accent on [1]**e** in this small fount, cf. 212 **hée** and 213 **thrée**

113 **nie**]e small fount   117 **times**]e indistinct   132 **bopit skil**]k incomplete, dirt on page before printing   138 **facions**

141 **p ride**   146 [1]**more**]m faint   156 **fuch e**]e ?small fount

170 **enteth**   194 **thy**] top of **t** damaged   195 **may gaines**

214 **althoug instruméth.**   237 **that**]a damaged

261 **buttous**   297 **you**] ℂ omitted   306 **feeing**] [1]**e** faint, possibly smaller fount   320 **welcome.**] stop indistinct, perhaps a comma   322 **thon**   323 **thon**   343 **cake**] damaged **c** or **t**

344 **your**]y small fount   360 **plead**]e indistinct   361 **gine**

379 **fighteh**   390 **knaue**]u indistinct   432 **falfheft**

433 **trowe**]o incomplete   461 **entice**] [1]**e** small fount

471 **he**] ℂ omitted   481 **borhe**   500 **he**] ℂ omitted

503 **Ma**] ℂ omitted   505 **thee**] [1]**e** faint, perhaps smaller fount

541 **dauucing**   561 **a fléep**   565 **letice**   596 **fnche**

618 **Nicholnewfangle**   673 **whorefaid**   675 [2]**thou**]u indistinct

698 **plat**   699 **cut purfe**] perhaps to match **cut throtes**

745 **liue: yet**   754 **By**] ℂ omitted   757 **J**] ℂ omitted

759 **J**] ℂ omitted   762 **My**] ℂ omitted   780 **him**]m marked or damaged   784 **likealway**   789 ?**pnrfe**

797 ?ttne uncertain   801 Meet]t ill-formed   803 three] [2]e

804 o ut   826 chat   836 their]t indistinct

851 with]t damaged   857 not]o small fount, or damaged

892 all] [1]l wrong fount   895 seemeth]eth not inked fully

936 Seing]¶ omitted   983 Piecre   1032 deuide] [2]d not fully inked   1040 eat]t indistinct, perhaps r   1043 catchword He should be This   1048 ⟨Ni. Ne⟩w] w damaged   no]o not fully inked   1064 roisting   1077 respect] [1]e incomplete

1101 pray]a faint   1108 b fore] [1]e missing   1120 entreth ,

1129 Iudexsi] si slightly dropped   1140 to   1172 begot

1205 hew   1215 hast]h not fully inked   1232 hane

1236 desireth] [1]e not fully inked   1252 leadeth]e, or damaged e

1271 haunce]un blotted   1282 curpurse   1325 thp

1335 catchword omitted   1339 There]¶ partly torn away

1353 hartes]es added by hand   1364 In]I obscured by fold

during repair to this leaf

4. Selected readings from Q2 and Q3. Q3 agrees with Q2, except where noted.

41 for] omitted Q2   43 of]and of Q2   73 me]him Q2

81 shall]wil Q2   87 vnto]to Q2   90 with]and Q2

94 you be]ye me not Q2   108 in]on Q3   146 [2]more]

omitted Q2   150 thou]that thou Q2   153 knowest]

knowest that Q2   167 suche]such a Q2   181 doost]doost

thou Q2   189 thy]Q3; the Q2   246 tail]tailes Q2

305 now]omitted Q2   306 that]omitted Q2   308 thou

maiſt]you may Q2   327 our]your Q2   388 your]you
your Q2   429 ²of]on Q2   505 good] omitted Q2
568 It]There Q2   589 that] omitted Q2   612 now]
omitted Q2   644 ſe ſhortly]ſhortly ſee Q2   664 and]
omitted Q2   695 any] omitted Q2   717 a] omitted Q2
721 as] omitted Q2   735 ²in] omitted Q2   745 to]in Q2
759 ²my] omitted Q2   787 ²doo]wil Q2   831 my]
mine Q2   854 worthy]Q3; worth Q2   860 am I]I am Q2
for] omitted Q2   878 thy] omitted Q2   881 him]me Q2
891 thank]thanks Q2   893 I doo therto]therto I doo Q2
908 you]thee Q2   909 from]Q3; of Q2   926 place]this
place Q2   940 doo thereto]therto do Q2   946 catchword
Good]Who Q2   962 in] omitted Q2   967 ſo] omitted Q2
978 for] omitted Q2   981 a] omitted Q2   1006 the] omitted
Q2   1012 is it now]it is Q2   1043 catchword he]This Q2
1044 he ſhall]thou ſhalt Q2   1048 where]whether Q2
1063 conſider]conſider this Q2   1073 all]all ye Q2; all you Q3
1076 youthly]youthful Q2; youthfull Q3   1095 now]not Q2
1101 pray]pray ye Q2   1103 or] omitted Q2   1107 his]the Q2
1109 that]this Q2   1143 meet]need Q2   1153 regard
neither]not regard Q2   1175 no]no more Q2   1220 a]
omitted Q2   1230 his] omitted Q2   1232 and]Q3; omitted
Q2   1306 may]can Q2   nor no]ne Q2   1307 catchword
haue]For Q2   1313 now] omitted Q2   1314 gracious]
verteous Q2; vertuous Q3   1335 catchword omitted]A Song Q2
1358 to bée]agree Q2